Looks Good on Paper?

LOOKS GOOD

on PAPER?

*Using In-Depth Personality Assessment
to Predict Leadership Performance*

LESLIE S.
PRATCH

Columbia University Press
Publishers Since 1893
New York   Chichester, West Sussex
cup.columbia.edu

Library of Congress Cataloging-in-Publication Data

Pratch, Leslie S.
Looks good on paper? : using in-depth personality assesment to predict
leadership performance / Leslie S. Pratch.
pages cm. — (Columbia business school publishing)
Includes bibliographical references and index.
ISBN 978-0-231-16836-6 (cloth: alk. paper) — ISBN 978-0-231-53764-3 (e-book)
1. Leadership—Psychological aspects. 2. Executive ability. 3. Personality assessment.
4. Executives—Psychology. 5. Executives—Selection and appointment. I. Title.

BF637.L4P656 2014
658.4'0920287—dc23

2013049165

Columbia University Press books are printed on permanent and durable acid-free paper.
This book is printed on paper with recycled content.
Printed in the United States of America

c 10 9 8 7 6 5 4 3 2 1

Cover design: Fifth Letter

Contents

Contents

Looks Good on Paper?

Introduction

LOOKS GOOD ON PAPER? operates on two levels. It speaks immediately to those who select leaders and to their advisers. Although traditional selection criteria based on past performance and achievements are indispensable, they do not adequately predict how a high-achieving person will handle new, unanticipated crises or, more generally, how anybody will perform in a new leadership role (e.g., as a CEO and not "just" a COO). A depth-psychological analysis, though not fully predictive, can close the gap significantly. *Looks Good on Paper?* describes a depth-psychological approach to assessment based on psychoanalytic insights and, in particular, how a psychological quality called "active coping" contributes powerfully to effective business leadership.

On another level, it speaks to a much wider audience. Individuals who have nothing to do with selecting leaders but who read this book merely out of curiosity or general interest are likely to come away with insights into their life and character and the lives and characters of those around them that they had not considered before—nothing conclusive or curative, but insights, questions, maybe more unexpected puzzles than answers, thought provoking and sometimes unsettling.

Equally important is what *Looks Good on Paper?* is not trying to do. It is not a general introduction to the subject of predicting leadership, a treatise for the Harvard Business School Library, or a textbook on management selection. It does not discuss different depth-psychological approaches and techniques. Above all, it does not claim that the approach I describe is better or more successful than others. Rather, it attempts to introduce readers to the subject by a highly personal account of my methods, findings, successes, and failures.

Leaders and leadership have always intrigued me. As a professional psychologist, I earn my living, among other activities, by making in-depth psychological assessments of senior managers, comparing candidates with impressive careers and trying to determine which one will function best in a given position. As I studied these executives and made these assessments, I arrived at some answers to the questions that plagued me from the start. Using data gathered in more than twenty years of experience, I have developed a methodology—the Active Coping Assessment System (which I will refer to later as my assessment system)—for predicting leadership not merely on one project or in one position but over the span of a career.

The focus of *Looks Good on Paper?* is on understanding the personality qualities of effective leaders, with a specific emphasis on business executives. Effective leaders are likely to act with consistently high integrity and to demonstrate sound, timely judgment when they occupy positions of power. The executives I examine are often similar in terms of general background and temperament. But every executive is unique. They may differ in terms of family background, work history, intellectual ability, and some overt behaviors. But the most striking differences, though not obvious or immediately apparent, are in their *underlying motivations* and their *coping tendencies*. Assuming a sustained motivation to lead others, it is the potential for "active coping" as I have defined it that is central to predicting effective leadership.

My approach to predicting leadership is only *one* example of new work in this field. There are others investigating these concepts, each according to his or her methods. I will not use this book as a forum to compare my methods to theirs; I will mostly focus on my own research and experiences.

I started down my current path while still at Northwestern University studying for a Ph.D. in clinical psychology. My area of focus was personality and leadership. In 1991, the dean of the University of Chicago's Graduate School of Business (now called the Booth School of Business and hereafter "Booth") asked me to lead research into the personality predictors of leadership. As the principal investigator, I designed and directed research on predicting which of the school's MBA students who were selected to participate in an elite leadership-development program would emerge as the most successful leaders. I worked with two such groups of students participating in this highly prestigious program from April 1990 until June 1994. Based on the strength of the findings of this study, the school funded a second study to see if we could replicate the results. We did and published the findings in peer-reviewed academic journals.[1]

This research became the basis of my Ph.D. dissertation at Northwestern University and motivated me to broaden my base of knowledge. To understand the business world better, I went on to earn an MBA at the University of Chicago, focusing on two areas about which I had known next to nothing before: strategy and finance.

I have continued doing academic work, publishing in a number of journals, including the *Journal of Applied Behavioral Science* and the *Journal of Private Equity*. But since 1998 I have been earning my living as a psychologist advising private equity investors, corporate directors, and senior executives of both public and privately held companies. In this capacity, I have, among other things, conducted in-depth assessments of more than four hundred current or potential CEOs or other senior executives.

The executives I assess are all holders of or finalists for senior leadership roles. And they are not unknowns. If the company is promoting from within, a great deal is known about the candidate. If a search firm presents candidates from the outside, it will have interviewed prospects, done extensive reference checking, and discreetly found out as much about each candidate as an experienced search professional can uncover. My clients call me in only when they have reduced the number of candidates still in the running to three, two, or even just one.

What my assessment adds is insight into the psychological qualities that distinguish one highflier from another. The assessment is particularly designed to predict how well a candidate is likely to cope with unexpected and unanticipated circumstances, to which past performance and personality are not always a good guide. I am sure you can think of more than a few examples of leaders who started with good records of past achievement and then surprised in either direction—some (like President Harry Truman) by their unexpected success, others (like Lincoln's first general in chief, George McClellan) by their unexpected failure to cope.

It is important for me to get some sense of potential new problems that might face the business so that the assessment can focus on the qualities needed to cope with them. For example, George Fisher had been an outstanding leader at Motorola, which he kept on the leading edge of technology. But he resigned as CEO of Kodak after almost six years because of his failure to transform it into a high-tech, growth-oriented company.

Fisher was very successful at Motorola. Motorola thrived by developing new technology that provided clear, significant advantages over old products and that often was sold first to businesses, where price was of less concern. It was noted for the speed with which it got new products to market. While Fisher was in senior management there, Motorola invented Six Sigma, emphasizing quality, production efficiencies, and hence successful and rapid time to market. Before becoming CEO of Motorola, just two years after Six Sigma's invention, Fisher extolled the Bandit team, a highly successful group of employees who designed, manufactured, and marketed a pager in record time, as the gold standard for all to follow. While he was there, Motorola's culture was nimble, dynamic, and flexible. Fisher thrived in that culture, and the company thrived under his leadership.

Kodak was a different organization. It was a mass marketer primarily of consumer products, so its existing and potential customers could be more selective in adopting pricey new products. It was famous for having good technology and good quality but also for being slow to get new products to market. That was fine when cameras and related products were new in the mass market, and Kodak dominated its market for many years. Not surprisingly, it became set in its ways, with a self-satisfied and inflexible bureaucracy.

By the time Fisher took over, Kodak faced stiff competition. It lacked the mindset of Motorola's Six Sigma culture, which valued quality, execution, and speed to market. Younger, nimbler competitors hammered Kodak on all fronts. Ferocious competition from Japanese companies such as Fuji, Sony, and Canon and Hewlett-Packard and other U.S. rivals more accustomed to the incredibly fast pace of change in digital technology required of Kodak a faster, more aggressive willingness to make changes and cut costs.

Fisher, with his great success at Motorola, was brought in to fix Kodak's problems, to reverse Kodak's earnings slide by reengineering the culture. He failed. The old-line manufacturing culture, which was not focused on execution, impeded his efforts to turn Kodak into a high-tech growth company. For example, despite Fisher's cost-cutting efforts, four years into his tenure at Kodak, its overhead expenses, at 27.6 percent of sales, remained higher than those of most of its competitors. The number of employees at continuing operations had grown by three thousand. Earnings and market share continued to slide.

In the nearly six years he was at Kodak, Fisher did not effectively address Kodak's problems. How could this happen? The most serious issues that continued to plague Kodak under Fisher—muddled marketing, a bloated cost structure, ever-growing competition, and, with respect to exports, a strong dollar—were either present for years or could have been anticipated. Kodak needed a leader who was willing and able to shake up the organization and its bureaucracy. Fisher was not willing and able to do that, at least not to the extent necessary to restore Kodak to its days of glory. He was slow to address Kodak's corporate culture, which remained mired in a mindset left over from an earlier manufacturing age. He did not shake up Kodak's bureaucracy as quickly and deeply as was needed and seemed averse to taking other aggressive, painful steps to cut costs and improve production processes.

Trying to nurture growth in both the analog and digital worlds at the same time may have been Kodak's greatest challenge. Fisher, in keeping with Kodak's tradition, wanted to balance the needs of its revenue- and profit-generating film business with new investments in digital technology, but the fear of cannibalizing its product lines slowed the company's growth in both the analog and digital spaces. At the same time, companies such as Hewlett-Packard, Canon, and Epson were aggressively producing competing products at ever-lower prices, and Kodak, despite Fisher's digital strategy and immersion in Six Sigma at Motorola, had trouble developing products that used the newest technology, much less taking them to market successfully.

An assessment might have shown that in spite of his glowing record at Motorola Fisher would not be the right CEO for Kodak. But it would have had to take consciously into account that Motorola and Kodak were radically different organizations, at far different stages of development, operating in strikingly different marketplaces, and facing far different challenges. It would then have asked whether he possessed the underlying psychological qualifies, such as the guts and aggression to act on his understanding of Kodak's problems, needed to reengineer Kodak. In sum, an assessment of Fisher might have exposed that for all of his outstanding qualities, Fisher was unlikely to work out as Kodak's savior. But this example shows that one needs to assess both the candidate and the complexities of the business in order to avoid such a mismatch.

I should make it clear that my assessments are not always one-shot affairs. The candidate assessed, if hired, receives an opportunity to review the assessment findings with me. At times, this review leads the executive to a period of self-evaluation and requests for coaching or repeat assessments to gauge his or her progress. An executive who comes to me privately receives a report of the findings of the assessment and in-depth feedback, which may lead to coaching regarding the inner preoccupations that led him to me in the first place.

Since 2004, I have continued to track the performance of executives I have assessed.[2] The partners or leaders of the firm commissioning the assessment are responsible for defining performance. In general, they usually rely on a combination of factors: return on invested capital, year-to-year growth, and data about the executives' performance—how they performed, whether they were promoted, how their fellow workers thought of them, and so on. Since starting my database in 2004, in order to hone my approach and identify areas where my predictions may fail, I have systematically interviewed the parties who commissioned the assessments every six months, twelve months, and two, three, four, five, six, and seven years—however long the executive is employed by a portfolio company or by the party that commissioned the assessment. I ask them how the executive has performed relative to the assessment indicators in my report. I ask for any surprising behaviors not indicated in the report. Their answers have bolstered my confidence in my assessment system, indicating predictive validity more than 98 percent of the time. The evidence they use is their firsthand experience working with the hired candidate and occasionally reports from others on the management team.

It's not just for my own use that I perform these follow-ups—they also have proved to be helpful to my clients: they force them to monitor more closely the chosen executive on an ongoing basis. These reviews are something they may want but would often fail to do without my prodding. They can then turn to me and my original assessment for help understanding how to handle an executive whose performance is not up to par.

My assessments are not black and white. Even the best candidates will be stronger in some situations and weaker in others, and my assessments attempt to bring that out. As my clients work with their new executives and find that they are indeed weaker in some situations, my assessments often help the clients and the executives understand why this is so and take appropriate steps to help the executives do their best work, which may even involve adjusting their direct responsibilities. And this, in turn, increases the chances that the investment will succeed.

Two caveats: First, as mentioned above, my practical experience, and thus my evidence for much of this book, is based on a small sample within a highly selective portion of the U.S. population. This sample consists mostly of executives or professionals who are being considered for upper management positions. They are all bright, ambitious, and successful by ordinary standards. They are mostly baby boomers, in their late thirties through mid-fifties at the time of assessment. They are mostly men. Because my sample group is limited, some of the findings and conclusions may not apply to other groups. I have no evidence as to how my findings would apply even to a similar group in a different culture, for example, to business executives in France or to political leaders in India. I do think, however, that the insights I've gained through the assessment can be instructive across the board in understanding what makes for a good leader and what qualities can help bolster effectiveness. I take a look at how these findings relate to female leaders in the final chapter of part 1.

Second caveat: It would be impractical to assess executives who might have been effective but who do not pass the résumé screen used to generate lists of potential candidates. My database is truly limited to executives who look good on paper. The assessment system is not best suited for catching candidates with less than stellar resumes, such as Ulysses S. Grant, one of the characters discussed in chapters 1, 6, 7, and 8. If for some reason the candidate has stayed alive through the vetting process, I can catch those who are less likely to perform well in the role for which they are being assessed and those who are more likely to perform well. But there are far more candidates who may have been effective but who do not pass the résumé screen and therefore fail to be considered for the job. Also, I have no way of knowing whether those whom I assessed as having a lower probability of success and who were rejected would have been successful in the role for which they were considered.

Looks Good on Paper? is organized into three parts. The first part focuses on active coping. Chapter 1 describes active coping and its elements, introducing it as a structural psychological construct and considering the corresponding implications for assessing personality as a complex structure. Chapter 2 illustrates how active coping—or lack thereof—affects an executive's performance. Chapter 3 describes the active coping style as demonstrated by two individuals and the passive coping style as demonstrated by Ernest Hemingway, presents the concept of "holes" in otherwise robust coping structures, and provides an illustrative story of an active coping executive with such a "hole" in his coping structure. Chapter 4 discusses my assessment approach, including the levels of personality assessed and how psychologists can ferret out executives who possess robust, active coping personality structures from those with holes in their coping structures, blind spots, and underlying passivity. Each of chapters 5 through 8 expands on one of the four elements of active coping: integrity in chapter 5, psychological autonomy in chapter 6, integrative capacity in chapter 7, and catalytic coping in chapter 8. Chapter 9 discusses coping issues relating to women in leadership roles.

The second part offers advice on self-assessment and development. Chapter 10 gives a general introduction on how to assess and strengthen your own active coping patterns. Chapter 11 provides a method for a thorough self-assessment and development regimen that can create a basis for strengthening one's active coping. Chapter 12 looks at one success story, a leader who was able to hone and strengthen his coping style.

The third part of the book is a companion for readers interested in more technical aspects of the research, model, methods, and measures. It delves deeper into the techniques used to uncover the subtle differences between highly functioning candidates who all look good on paper, outlines a structural psychological model of personality, and describes the psychoanalytic origins of the theory of active coping. It also expands on the research methods and findings.

PART I

The Theory and Practice
of Active Coping

I

The Power of Active Coping

THE CORPORATE WORLD IS a highly charged, ever-changing cru-
cible. Leaders in it are sorely tested. There are other arenas just
as tough—the military and politics, to give two examples. In the
wake of the 2008 economic meltdown, many of us have been
asking the same questions that I have been exploring for years. Is
it possible to predict which executives are potential time bombs,
to learn to tell a young Warren Buffett from a young, merely
competent investment banker? And is it possible to help executives understand how some aspects of their personalities could
adversely affect performance at work or which an awareness of
might help them modify their behavior? I believe that it is possible
to make such predictions with a fair degree of accuracy, and this
book discusses how I have tried to do that.

An effective leader must meet challenges and resolve them pro-
ductively, day after day. He or she must constantly adapt to the
unforeseen—and must mobilize, coordinate, and direct others. But
when hiring executives, how do you know which candidates possess such qualities? When they all look good on paper, how do you

make a choice? How do you get past the résumé to perceive the person and, most important, predict the performance? To give some specific examples: Who would have predicted from the twenty-year tenure of David Pottruck at Schwab that he would fail so miserably as the handpicked, groomed successor to founder Charles Schwab? Or, similarly, that Doug Ivestor at Coke would fail when he followed the famed CEO Roberto Goizetta? How could organizations avoid hiring charismatic yet ultimately value-destroying leaders like Jeff Kindler, first at McDonalds and then at Pfizer?

An executive's failure adversely affects many individuals and organizations. The company loses money: Firing an executive may incur legal and severance fees, the cost of recruiting and developing a replacement, and losses from interrupted schedules or abandoned projects. Dismissing a senior executive can cause upheaval and chaos among the company's employees. It may even affect the board of directors if its members are personally blamed for the executive's poor decisions. As productivity drops, the effect may trickle down to the company's clients or suppliers, eventually hurting the surrounding communities. As we have seen in recent years, our economy tightly weaves together many seemingly unconnected business sectors.

Active Coping

As one approach to help organizations avoid the adverse effects of poor leadership, I have continued to develop the theory of active coping. The theory is explained more scientifically in other publications and in the technical companion to chapter 4 (appendix B).[1] I also look individually at each element of active coping in chapters 5 through 8. Here, I describe it as it appears in everyday life.

Even if you have never heard the term, you know it when you see it. When a person always seems prepared and quickly recovers from any setback, that is active coping. When a person earns the trust of her friends and colleagues by refusing to take unfair advantage of others and refuses to let others take unfair advantage of her, that is active coping. When a person has the vision and self-confidence to rise above "business as usual" when necessary, that is active coping. When a person is open to the people around her, listens to bad as well as good news, and is aware of her own motivations, strengths, and shortcomings, that is active coping.

To many, the word "cope" has connotations of barely scraping by. I use it quite differently, to refer to a sense of mastery, an orientation to life. All human beings encounter difficulties on a daily basis, both internal (to the self) and external. We have intricate internal landscapes filled with drives, values, dreams, and ideals. Some are compatible and some are in conflict. "Coping" is how we reconcile and express these many parts of ourselves, endeavoring to bring into balance our internal needs and the external demands of our environment. Individuals can learn to master themselves and the circumstances that surround them, taking an active coping stance toward the world. Or they can be passive copers, allowing themselves to be defined by their circumstances and enslaved by their personal needs. When circumstances change unpredictably, an individual's latent weaknesses—or untested strengths—emerge.

We all have to make an effort to achieve our goals. To do so, we usually have to solve problems and overcome obstacles. Some are created by our surroundings, some by other people, and some by who we are. Encountering these obstacles creates stress. When we take action—whether cognitive or behavioral—to reduce that stress, we are coping. Coping is part of the process of adapting to and even changing the environment.

When dealing with stress, a person can respond in one of four ways. The first is to identify the stress and remove it, maintaining— even improving— physical and emotional health. The second is to identify and tolerate the stress without changing it, keeping the status quo but not growing. The third is to defend against the stress by denying it, distorting the perception of it, or reacting to it in an unrealistic manner. The fourth is to suffer a complete breakdown in functioning. The first response is active coping. The second response is passive coping. The third response is neurotic, defensive coping. The fourth response accompanies personality disintegration.

What Is Active Coping?

Active coping is the healthiest response to stressful situations and the one most likely to lead to a successful resolution. It is like a car: We can manage to get where we need to go if we are driving an ordinary, inexpensive car, and we can make it through life with a less than optimal coping style. But driving a car with superb engineering is crucial if we are racing in the Indianapolis 500 and will get us farther, faster, with less likelihood of accident or breakdown in other situations. A strong framework of coping does exactly the same thing.

Active coping is the readiness, willingness, and ability to adapt resourcefully and effectively to novel and changing conditions. It is a stable, albeit complex psychological orientation across time and circumstance, a style of functioning, a continuous seeking for the most effective path through life. Think of it as a constant state of being "open for business" that springs from a healthy personality structure. It comes into play in the now, at each moment of decision or challenge.

Individuals who are active copers strive to achieve personal aims and overcome difficulties rather than passively retreat or become overwhelmed. The psychological ammunition that active coping provides is extremely useful when determining the best way to respond to a situation that was not, or could not be, anticipated. Active copers feed on experience; they incorporate what they have learned into their psychological systems, making themselves increasingly capable of tolerating uncertainty and devising new strategies for growth. When they fail, they learn why and respond more effectively the next time. Rather than hide from constructive criticism, they seek it out as useful advice. This openness increases their effectiveness as leaders and, more generally, in life.

Active copers support others and take advantage of opportune moments to share what they have learned. They pass on their experiences not only to help others make similar improvements but to remind themselves of their own life lessons and reinforce their own growth. This tendency to teach and share is what motivates leaders to develop mentoring relationships, helping younger, up-and-coming leaders develop their own modes of active coping.

Whereas active copers seek to confront and resolve challenges, passive copers are reactive and avoidant. Passive coping is an inability to tolerate the full tension of a difficult situation. We have all seen examples of passive coping: the board member who reacts in crisis before the CEO can gather sufficient facts, the manager who lashes out at subordinates to relieve stress, or the friend who hides from tough decisions. Passive coping is retreating from reality, tuning out information, and resisting change. It's dealing with minor problems in order to avoid confronting the anxiety of major problems. It's rearranging the deck chairs on the *Titanic*. In business, active copers continue to build their understanding of industry dynamics and disruptive technologies and to anticipate economic changes; passive copers repeat what worked yesterday.

Active copers are not always successful. Any number of unexpected events—injury or illness, economic downturns, divorce, war, the competition, disruptive technologies—may undo good planning and resolute effort. Reality is essentially refractory. It gets in the way of what we want. Even when life does not throw up insurmountable barriers, we can fail. No one copes actively in every situation. We don't expect perfection of those around us and shouldn't expect it of ourselves. But knowing that sometimes our coping may falter, we can take steps to prevent it. Shoring up weaknesses is a part of active coping, too.

This book is about more than active coping in business, but it focuses on active coping in business leaders. Leaders, by the nature of their position, have to cope not only with their personal goals and frustrations but with the goals and frustrations of their followers and the group as a whole. To be effective and reliable, leaders must be capable of active coping. Leaders must be persistent; good leadership is not merely handling one problem effectively but handling a multitude of problems well and recovering quickly from setbacks with energy and determination to prevail. Leaders must also be flexible, able to adapt resourcefully and rapidly to current and potential crises. These qualities of flexibility, adaptability, creativity, and endurance are fundamental to active coping.

Active coping as an overall style of functioning enables us to meet the demands of the external world as well as our internal needs without letting one overwhelm the other. When we bring the two into harmony, we experience self-esteem, contentment, and happiness. When we adapt to the external world in a way that makes us feel good about ourselves, we get the energy to continue to grow and adapt.

Leaders who possess healthy, integrated personalities can tolerate the tension felt when handling challenges, threats, or conflicts. They can create and implement strategies to overcome challenges, deal with threats, and resolve conflicts. These strategies operate consciously and unconsciously in such a way that brings into balance environmental pressures and individual aspirations, needs, and values. This balancing act is particularly important for leaders because their functioning affects all who are touched by their leadership. A leader must be a whole person with strong active coping in order to meet the responsibilities of leading. Active coping is what we *expect* from leaders: the readiness and ability to learn, adapt, improvise, mobilize, and overcome conflicts. Leaders who possess these qualities are far more likely to be effective than those who do not.

Because leadership has long-term implications, my focus is on making long-term (e.g., three- to ten-year) predictions. I choose to look at coping not as a one-time effort but as a style, a constant state of readiness that supports healthy growth and adaptation over the course of a person's life. Just as investors evaluate a company to understand its earning potential, I assess an executive or potential executive to predict his or her potential to grow and perform in a specific role.[2] Identifying a candidate's coping style forms the core of my evaluation process but not its full extent. My evaluation process also takes into account the interactions of the executive, the corporate strategy, and the operating environment. Each situation is unique, but knowing the effects of each component with a high degree of detail strengthens the ability to predict whether executives will perform as required.

Four Elements of Active Coping

I developed the psychological model of leadership by studying both the theories behind the concept of active coping and the qualities required for effective leadership.[3] I thought about what effective leaders did, felt, and thought; why they behaved as they did; why they made the decisions they made; and why those actions were effective—or not. I condensed these thoughts and theories down to create my personal definition of effective leadership: *leadership is effective when it influences the actions of followers toward the achievement of the goals of the group or organization.* Working with this definition, I identified four interconnected parts, four elements of the active coping style: integrity, psychological autonomy, integrative capacity, and catalytic coping. These elements seemed necessary to engender and sustain effective leadership.[4]

Integrity depends on the consistency of behavior in accordance with values and ideals.[5] Leaders who demonstrate integrity earn the trust of their followers, their superiors, and the community.

This trust allows them to function more efficiently because they don't have to spend a long time getting acceptance and approval for each action they take. Lack of integrity causes leaders to act erratically because they are not strongly connected to a secure or consistent system of values. They are unreliable leaders, often favoring their personal whims over the interests of others, and may damage their organizations or communities by their selfish actions.

Psychological autonomy involves the ability to recognize and respect the aims and feelings of others while purposefully striving to achieve a goal or path. It is the ability to make and impose choices on the world—the opposite of groupthink. Psychological autonomy gives a person the freedom to choose the most effective course of action.[6] Leaders with high psychological autonomy can respectfully disagree with their followers, their colleagues, and their superiors. They have the confidence to take an unpopular but necessary action and stand firm against doubt and disapproval. Conversely, those with low psychological autonomy capitulate to pressure from their subordinates, peers, and authority figures. They require the safety of consensus.

Integrative capacity is an ingrained ability, developed through practice, to draw together diverse elements of a complex situation into a coherent pattern. It is, literally, the capacity to integrate information from one's self and surroundings into a new and greater understanding of the tapestry of life.[7] Leaders with strong integrative capacity are aware of their emotions and motivations as well as their weaknesses. They have open minds, accepting input from all sources. Then they put together what they know about themselves with the realities of their situations to create a deep understanding of possibilities. Leaders with poor integrative capacity have a narrow focus, ignoring any information that doesn't fit their limited worldview. They may have little awareness of their own motivations and states of mind and therefore fail to understand the motivations of others. They lack an understanding of mutuality. They deal with events one at a time, blind to the connections between them, unable to extrapolate into the future.

Catalytic coping is the ability to invent creative, effective solutions to problems and then carry them out. It is the most overt expression of active coping, the easiest to observe and measure. Leaders strong in catalytic coping always seem to have thought out several options to resolve each problem. If there isn't an option, they create one. They develop detailed plans and execute them. That does not mean they are rigid; if conditions change and the plan ceases to be effective, catalytic copers immediately rethink their options and adjust the plan. Leaders who lack catalytic coping do not look, think, or plan ahead. If they come up with a plan, it often lacks depth or creativity. They will stick to it whether it suits current conditions or not. They seem lost when faced with difficult or unusual conditions and may fail to take timely action or any action at all.

These are not entirely different factors; they are elements of a whole style of being. If you wonder whether the four elements of active coping carry different weights in predicting leadership effectiveness or general adaptation to life, consider this analogy: Are there relative weights for the circulatory, respiratory, digestive, endocrine, and neurological systems of the body? One could argue that one system is more crucial than another—but the fact is that if any of those systems ceased to operate, the body would die. If any became relatively dysfunctional, such dysfunction would affect the entire body. In the same way, the four elements of active coping rely on one another to function effectively.

Another good analogy is a Greek temple—solid, stable, enduring. The building's strong pillars support a wide triangular pediment and roof; intact, it can withstand nature's onslaught for centuries. This iconic structure illustrates well how the elements of active coping are a crucial part of active coping as a whole. Each element—integrity, psychological autonomy, integrative capacity, and catalytic coping—is like a pillar. Each supports the active

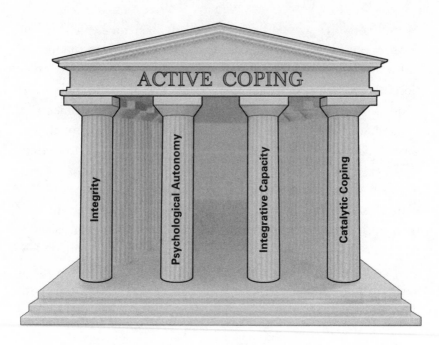

FIGURE 1.1 The Elements of Active Coping

coping "roof," which covers and encompasses them all. If one pillar is missing, the structure loses stability and strength. If more than two pillars are missing, the structure crumbles. But if all four pillars are in place, the structure will stand firm for many years. I look for this active coping structure when I am trying to identify executive candidates who will stand the test of time in a challenging position.

Speaking directly about coping, the ultimate goal of successful adaptation and growth depends on the operations and interaction of the four elemental functions. Basically, a person has to take in stimuli (from the outer and inner worlds), make reality-oriented sense of those stimuli (integrative capacity), be relatively free to derive possible strategies of response (psychological autonomy), and execute those strategies (catalytic coping) while remaining true to ethical (social and external) and personal (organismic and internal) guidelines and needs (integrity and self-esteem). Dysfunctions in any area can generate maladaptive processes and results in the area in question or across areas as other areas try to respond or compensate.

Using another example, with the Chicago Blackhawks in 2013's summer headlines, sports teams optimize functioning when players of all positions perform maximally. Any player who plays poorly will cause weaknesses in the team effort and likely impair the team's chances of winning. The ultimate result will be a function of which team positions are most affected and how the remaining positions react and try to compensate.

When choosing a leader, I believe that the first step is for the board to define in specific, rigorous terms what it will take for a candidate to succeed in the role. I require that my clients specify exactly what they want in a CEO, particularly the specific skills and relationships the company will need most, before conducting a search. What are the unique and specific role requirements for the company and for a successful CEO in the operating environment at that time? Some requirements are just that: requirements that are necessary and irrevocable.

In addition, given today's increasingly uncertain business environment, a CEO should possess the nonnegotiable qualities of character, including integrity, and a strong record of bringing about large-scale change and customer orientation, as well as business acumen (the ability to diagnose what ails or could potentially ail the company and to envision how to improve it, and the ability to execute needed change and take the company forward).

In short, after rigorously defining the current and potential future business environment, when choosing a leader, four basic criteria should be met. A leader must have the interpersonal skills to lead, the intuitive intelligence to lead, the motivation to lead, and the active coping structure to support the first three criteria. There are plenty of off-the-shelf tools in use today that measure the first two criteria—some accurately, many inaccurately—but few that measure the latter two. An in-depth psychological assessment helps get a more accurate measurement of a leader's motivation and coping. As stated previously, active coping is a crucial psychological component of more observable skills that lead to good performance. It allows a leader to organize and amplify other leadership skills and develop new skills when the situation requires them.

The theory of active coping as I have developed it and its use in predicting leadership represent relatively new thinking in the area of leadership research. As noted earlier in this chapter, I refer to coping as an *attitude* or *style*, an overall approach to dealing with life's challenges, rather than the ability to handle one problem or stressor. This long-term, developmental focus is what makes the construct of active coping so useful in evaluating leaders. Leaders in real-world situations are required to overcome multiple complex and ongoing challenges, often in parallel rather than one at a time, and they are expected to do so for many years while continually improving their performance. Short-term definitions of coping are helpful for certain types of research, but they do not reflect coping style as individuals demonstrate it over the course of their lives.

Skills and Traits Associated with Active Coping

Active coping is an attribute of a healthy personality structure. That means that the "activity" is not always overt and observable; sometimes it takes place internally, in decisions made, visions developed, conflicting drives resolved. An active coping stance, however, often gives rise to certain observable traits and skills. These include the following:

- *Awareness.* Active copers are able to see reality, including their own needs, capabilities, and limitations.
- *Courage.* Active copers are brave. They seek out new experiences; they are not intimidated by challenges.

- *Resiliency, toughness, and the ability to learn from experience.* Active copers, like all humans, make mistakes. Life is too complicated to anticipate every possible contingency. After a setback, active copers regroup and recover.
- *Energy, fortitude, and the willingness to persevere.* Active copers summon their energy and continue to move forward even under the most trying circumstances.
- *Resourcefulness.* Active copers invent solutions to problems by creatively pulling together the resources they have at hand or by developing new resources.
- *Decisiveness.* Active coping gives a person the fortitude to handle conflicts among competing goals. Making a choice means giving up an alternative. Active copers face that loss and move on.
- *Executing a plan.* Active coping involves planning. Active copers anticipate, strategize, and weigh the risks of potential actions. Then they act. Active coping combines introspection and action.

It should be immediately apparent that many of these skills and traits overlap. You have to be aware of a problem before you can plan to overcome it. In order to make a good plan, you have to be resourceful. In order to carry it out, you may need courage. Because active coping is a characteristic of the whole person and its elements are not "traits" or "skills" in the narrow, common definition of those terms, you will see this sort of complexity and interconnectedness repeatedly throughout the book as I give real-life examples of active coping. It is one of the reasons that I emphasize the importance of a full assessment of the candidate, the position, and the organization when making predictions.

As adults, we have internalized the rules and structures of our society, but to babies, those rules are entirely external. Babies don't even know the rules exist until they get old enough to be aware of the constraints placed on them. Toddlers go through the "terrible twos" (and threes and fours) because their expression of their internal drives and desires comes into constant opposition from the structure of human society. As children grow up, their parents and authority figures impose the rules and structures of their culture on them, repeating the limitations and explaining the purpose of the appropriate behavior until the children accept the rules and can follow them independently. Susie's mother tells her, "No, Susie, don't grab that toy. Share with your brother." Susie learns that she gets approval for sharing. She learns to identify with her brother, and she also identifies with her parents in treating her brother as someone to take care of and treat empathically. But the values and ideals that she internalizes were initially experienced as limitations to the gratification of her basic desires by the external environment.

When we internalize society's rules, they become part of us, no longer something outside working contrary to our desires. We begin to develop a personal identity, where internal and external meet to become "us," the core of our being. Leaders who are active copers have integrated these conflicting impulses into a healthy, coherent, consistent whole.

The Many Dimensions of Personality

My work rests on four assumptions about personality.

One, personality is fundamentally a theoretical construct, not a concrete object that can be easily measured and discussed in absolutes. We use the concept of personality to explain how people think, feel, and act. We characterize personality in shorthand terms—Simon is warm and empathic; Julie, calculating and aloof—but such characterizations touch only on a few of the many parts that go into the makeup of the whole person. Although personality is conceptually rich and complex, it can be rigorously and scientifically assessed.

Two, with the right tools and training, we can predict the effects of personality on decision making.

Three, with concerted effort, often supported by psychotherapy, we can change certain aspects of our personality, but only to a limited degree. Our personalities are a function of our individual histories, especially our childhoods. This restricts the extent to which we are able to reshape ourselves. This limitation does not mean that change is impossible, of course, and in chapters 10 through 12 I look at how you, the reader, can develop your own leadership abilities and enhance your patterns of coping.

Four, our personalities operate at different levels of awareness: conscious, semiconscious, and unconscious. Each level affects how we think, feel, and act in ways that may not be obvious or easily measured.

We can think of personality as an iceberg. Just as the iceberg has different levels of submersion, our personalities have different levels of conscious awareness. What's above the surface of the ocean is easily visible. This is the conscious level, the part of our personalities over which we have complete control. We can see this obvious level in action. Deep below the ocean's surface is the unconscious level. That part of the iceberg we cannot see without special training and equipment. In between is the semiconscious level: we can vaguely make out what is just below the waterline. Much of our behavior is driven by what's below the surface, by the unconscious parts we don't see or understand. The unconscious influences the conscious just as the submerged part of the iceberg influences the tip above the water's surface.

Because we are mostly aware of the conscious level, the tip of the iceberg, we feel that we have full control of our actions, but sometimes we discover that we *don't* have control. We may do surprising things that may not be in our best interests for reasons we don't understand. We have deeper motives; we have hidden fears and wishes. The more aware we become of these unconscious dimensions of our personalities, the more likely it is that we

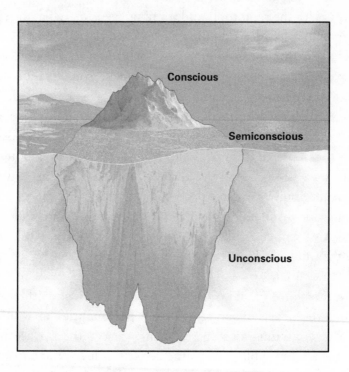

FIGURE 1.2 The Personality Iceberg

can master them. Getting in touch with our psychological makeup is important if we are to behave with appropriate flexibility and strength, the hallmarks of active coping. The better we cope, the greater our chances of being successful.

Implications for Assessing Personality

Active coping defined as a structural psychological attribute carries implications for assessing personality. Developmental models stem from a structural psychological approach. As will be discussed in chapter 4, such an approach taps levels of behavior that are difficult to observe. It allows psychologists to measure subtle distinctions among superficially similar individuals, adding substantial independent information that can reduce predictive errors in top management selection. The assessment process that I use specifically draws upon multiple facets of a candidate's public and private history. It measures various levels of psychological functioning from overt to covert, conscious to unconscious, to create a model of the whole person, including coping structure. The depth and coherence of this model adds substantially to the accuracy of predictions. It allows one to see what lies beneath—and its relevance to business leadership.

Coping style, to put it more simply, is a characteristic of personality as a whole. It is not an easily observable, easily measurable trait. Trait-based theories and models attempt to explain and predict an individual's way of thinking, feeling, acting, and reacting in a certain situation, with its specific characteristics and psychological significance, by combining values from a set of traits. Accounts are framed in terms of one major quality of the person at a time and only secondarily in terms of the relationships among these qualities. This approach characterized both the early trait studies and most of the current research on personality and leadership.[8] Pure trait models do not treat psychological functioning as a dynamic process, even when the importance of interactions among personality characteristics is noted.[9] A pure trait approach also cannot account for the coincidence of cohesiveness and stability, on the one hand, and creativity and flexibility, on the other, seen in effective leaders.[10]

The trait approach leaves several questions unanswered. Are these traits indeed different tendencies, or do they reflect an underlying personality (organismic) structure? How do attributes such as self-esteem, self-confidence, sociability, and intelligence relate to other individual characteristics, such as need for achievement, moral responsibility, regulation of affects and impulses, and an overall sense of "identity"? Do deficiencies in the latter undermine the degree to which the former can contribute to a leader's effectiveness?

To focus on traits or sets of knowledge, skills, and abilities without linking these to broader and more latent aspects of the individual's goal system is to divorce leadership style from issues of personality. Individuals do not function as disjointed collections of parts but as more or less coordinated wholes. Conceptually and empirically, examining each characteristic individually does not capture the full and unique functioning of the whole.

A Structural Psychological Model of Leadership

The model I use is based, as I've said, on the construct of "active coping." Active coping makes it possible to integrate and apply different skills or competencies to a changing environment. The utility of a specific competency depends on the situation; however, for leadership across multiple situations what is necessary is a global factor that permits the integration of multiple aspects of experience and self. This integrative capacity increases the possibility of acts of creative leadership. The greater the capacity for active coping, the more likely it becomes that the individual will exhibit the specific skills or high-level competencies that support effective leadership. In this sense, active coping can be seen as the "prime mover" of specific leadership competencies.

The following propositions summarize the particular structural model:

1. Active coping is a necessary determinant of leadership effectiveness. Active coping represents a general underlying factor that contributes to individual adaptation and growth in many areas besides leadership.[11] Active coping may represent an individual, generic, adaptive competency involving stress tolerance, affective regulation, and self-direction.

2. Active coping is not a sufficient determinant of leadership. Active coping as a single variable does not predict effective

leadership; other variables are also important. I am not stating that active coping will predict leadership. I am saying that effective leaders will tend to be active copers. In a pool of one hundred managers equally intelligent as measured by normal measure of IQ and equally motivated to ascend to senior management, individuals who are active copers are more likely to be effective than their passive coping counterparts.

3. Motivational orientation is a crucial determinant of a leadership style. Active copers who are not motivated to lead are unlikely to become leaders.[12] Active copers who have the internal motivation to teach math may well become excellent math teachers.

4. Successful leadership requires specific skills, abilities, and high-level competencies that operate in a cumulative and substitutable way. Examples include goal setting, sensitivity and empathy, the ability to persuade others to drop their opposition and help, the ability to anticipate problems and invent ways of surmounting them, the ability to overcome bureaucratic resistance to change, and the ability to effect compromise among warring factions.

5. The situation determines the extent to which a specific style or ability may be useful or necessary. This is the realm of contingency models. For example, a person may be an active coper yet may lack the motivation or knowledge needed to lead effectively in a given situation.

6. Combining active coping with specific motives and abilities provides a heuristic to explain the development of a leadership style. For example, assuming a base level of high intelligence, we can expect that active copers with high needs for affiliation, power, and a desire to nurture colleagues and subordinates will learn to relate to others with empathy, tact, and persuasiveness. The resulting leadership styles may resemble more participative styles. Conversely, active copers with high needs for achievement and autonomy may develop more authoritarian styles.

As it stands, the model is heuristic and suggests aspects of leadership that need further exploration. Chapter 9 presents one test of this model and demonstrates its empirical validity. Psychologists have developed operational strategies to assess the validity of these propositions and are continually examining them empirically. The benefit of the model lies in its power to enhance the abilities of organizations to identify and groom candidates for senior leadership roles.

2

Predicting Performance

Why is it every time I ask for a pair of hands, they come with a brain attached?

—HENRY FORD

HOW DOES UNDERSTANDING A leader's coping style aid in executive selection? Consider Abraham Lincoln's frustrating search for a capable army commander during the Civil War. He had his pick of generals with illustrious West Point backgrounds, and even generals who had shown great bravery and resourcefulness as juniors and senior officers in the Mexican-American War fifteen years earlier.

General George B. McClellan had a towering reputation going into the Civil War. He was a masterful raiser, organizer, and trainer of armies, and his men were fiercely loyal to him, but he proved a failure leading the Union Army in battle. Only when he had observed Ulysses S. Grant in action did Lincoln find a man capable of rising to the occasion. In 1864 Grant became overall army commander. Grant had been a failure in every trade he ever tried—tanner, farmer, soldier (he resigned as a captain well before the Civil War began), but there was one thing Grant could do better than any man of his time: He could lead an army to victory in war. A creative and relentless fighter, he won battle after battle until he had worked his way to the top. Could his success, or McClellan's failure, have been predicted?

Lincoln did not have the option to assess his generals using clinical psychological methods; he had to make choices knowing their overt strengths and weaknesses but not their covert, unconscious tolerance for stress. Using current methods to uncover his generals' coping structures, he might have gotten a more accurate picture of how they would handle the trauma of war. A thorough assessment would likely have caught McClellan's hesitation to act under pressure and Grant's underlying determination to push through against all odds. Although, as will be discussed in chapter 8, Grant was not effective in many situations, such as leading the country during peacetime, he was the right leader for the particular situation that had nearly destroyed the Union. His particular coping style made him the right military leader during wartime.

Most human beings are like Grant, thriving under some circumstances, faltering under others. As I mention repeatedly throughout this book, there is no such thing as a perfect coper, someone able to handle every problem at any time. All candidates for any role will have some flaws in their coping structure. An in-depth assessment helps the person making the assessment uncover and understand these coping flaws. Such information is crucial to making accurate predictions about leaders' long-term success. Knowing that they will flourish in one situation but wilt in another allows superiors—whether they are CEOs or presidents—to place leaders in positions that will play to their strengths and not their weaknesses. A large part of predicting leadership effectiveness is identifying the conditions under which a leader will be effective.

Making Predictions: Effectiveness Versus Success

When discussing leadership, it is important to differentiate the concept of effectiveness from that of success. Effectiveness means that the leader is able to gain the support of others and make progress toward the defined organizational goals. Success means that the goals are in fact achieved, and that may or may not be attributable to the leader's actions. It is also true that a failure to achieve the goals may not be the fault of the leader.

Leadership is effective when it influences the actions of followers toward the achievement of the goals of the group or organization. An effective leader directs the activities of followers and motivates them to carry out their duties efficiently. The rules, regulations, and processes of the larger organization influence the leader in performing these functions and may have a positive or negative impact on the leader's effectiveness.

At times, a group may be confronted with tasks for which no clearly defined goals or procedures exist. The leader and his or her followers must then define the group's goals and develop procedures for attaining these objectives. The leader performs the crucial synthetic functions of information processing as well as those functions that direct, control, and energize group activities.

A coach may optimize the performance of his team and create a clever strategy but still lose the game. The team may lose because the competition is more talented or more experienced or because a key athlete is injured. In business, even a well-regarded leader with deep industry expertise may not succeed when circumstances are unfavorable. Success is not an inevitable result of effective leadership. Conversely, a company may achieve success in the absence of good leadership from its management. It is possible for an executive to be ineffective yet successful thanks to an excellent support team, a strong economy, or other fortunate conditions.

The very definition of success may be quite different depending on who is doing the defining. One group might consider an outcome successful while another group considers it a failure. In a business setting, owners, board members, the CEO, other members of management, other employees, and individuals living in the local community might well have different goals and therefore define success differently.

For these reasons, it is impossible to predict the long-term success of any leader without the use of a time machine. It may be easier to gauge the probability of failure than the probability of success. Predictions about *effective* leadership are less subject to luck and perspective. A leader can continue to be effective even when the goal becomes more distant or changes altogether.

While my approach cannot make predictions about the potential *success* of an executive, it can and does make accurate predictions about an executive's potential to be an *effective* leader. For example, Charles and Henry were two adult men who were born into wealth. Eldest sons of high-socioeconomic-status families, growing up in New York City with fathers who were professionally successful, they earned degrees at first-rate colleges and graduate schools. Both married women with wealthy parents. Both were narcissists: they were extremely self-centered, unable to experience other persons as separate (from themselves) people with needs of their own. They surrounded themselves with subordinates who were hired on the basis of the subordinate's ability to mirror and capitulate to their demanding, autocratic leadership styles.

Neither Charles nor Henry, despite their material wealth, had been an effective *leader*. They may have been viewed as publicly successful because they had endowed educational institutions as a means of self-aggrandizement. But they were not respected by peers or subordinates and never built teams that succeeded in business. They were able to buy their way into power by investing money into funds that granted them majority shareholder rights. But the money they were able to invest they owed to their inherited wealth. Although superficially successful in terms of net worth and social status, they were ineffective as leaders. Henry, for example, tried to build a firm that ultimately rejected him—the individuals he brought in to be partners deplored his self-serving methods and moved to other firms or started their own. Henry's peers in the industry did not respect him. That lack of respect and the failure of his firm literally drove him out of the industry in the United States. Charles, though materially very successful and still a named officer of his firm, held a title but did not function in a leadership capacity.

Reducing Future Risk

The point of making predictions about leaders, whether they are generals, executives, or politicians, is to reduce the risk of failures in leadership. If Grant had failed, the history of our country would be radically different. Failures of many leaders in the financial industry and government contributed to a global economic crisis. The decisions that leaders make cause repercussions that flow outward into the world like ripples on a pond. Those charged with choosing leaders have a heavy responsibility.

Consider the dilemma of a group of investors looking for senior managers to lead companies in their portfolio. Predicting how candidates for senior management are likely to perform under conditions of high stress and uncertainty is one of the most fateful judgments for investors to make. Most are capable of evaluating the company's business and potential markets, and they recognize that the success of the company depends on the ability of the management team to deliver on those prospects. Yet, as will continue to be repeated in this section, many still hire leaders the way they did fifty years ago, thus assuming more risk than they realize. I believe that in-depth assessment systems, including the one described in this book, bring to the business world more effective, sophisticated methods and thus reduce that risk.

Investors and boards of directors have a forward-looking approach to evaluating technology and markets but often use a backward-looking approach to evaluating managers. They believe they can infer a great deal about future performance from an executive's career history, but past performance alone has proven to be a poor predictor of future functioning. Correlations between past and future functioning in the managerial population range between .3 and .5 at most, a finding well documented in the empirical research literature on leadership from the past sixty years.[1]

Executives with the greatest likelihood of performing successfully in senior management roles are those who can respond effectively to emergent, dynamic, and complex situations. This means that when investors or boards of directors choose executives for such roles, they should assess the executives' readiness to acquire new skills and strategies for coping with novelty: in other words, their active coping.

Of course, that doesn't mean that an active coper is ideal for every organization. If an organization is characterized by traditional and increasingly dysfunctional loyalties, then don't put an active coper in at any level. If you want to change a stagnant bureaucracy, then put in an active coper. An active coper would only want to become part of the Veterans Administration (at least as I came to know it during one rotation during my clinical training) if he knows that he has political support for transforming and modernizing the organization. If you want the organization to change, then you need someone with the innovation and drive of an active coper.

An executive's past performance is partially the result of happenstance, that is, factors extraneous to and uncontrolled by the executive. As the records of Grant and McClellan demonstrate, a leader's past success does not automatically imply the capacity to succeed in a new environment, nor does past failure imply future failure. How much is success a lucky outcome rather than the result of deliberate application of talent? How much is failure brought on by unfortunate and unavoidable circumstances?

When making an analysis, one must disentangle the role of unpredictable chance and circumstance from the executive's objective past and ongoing ability to function under conditions of challenging uncertainty (chapter 4 illuminates how clinical psychologists can make predictions about future, unknown conditions.) As we will see, I try to tease out the particular talents that worked for the executive in the past and discuss the circumstances under which those attributes may or may not work in the future.

For example, Alex had been a successful turnaround CEO. He had degrees from an Ivy League college and one of the top five MBA programs in the United States. He had a sustained marriage, a supportive wife, and wealth accumulated from his prior turnaround positions. A large venture capital firm hired him to be the managing partner of its early-stage information investments, one of two funds. Alex had never effectively operated within a partnership.

I assessed him at his request—not his firm's. He reported to me that he had attempted suicide as a child as part of a history of corrosive relationships beginning with his father and continuing with peers throughout his childhood, adolescence, college, and career and that he did not actually live in the same household as his wife. Because he had requested the assessment privately, the findings were not disclosed to any other party. I believe he recognized his psychological instability and wanted help but at a safe distance (i.e., "coaching") and, at the same time, support in altering the dynamics of the firm partnership so that he could call the shots rather than share power with the managing director of the firm's sister fund. The more I worked with Alex, the more I saw how he undermined relations with the sister fund, disparaging its managing director by challenging his decisions, questioning the validity of the data presented by his team, and creating friction between the two funds. Their disagreements became widely known throughout the firm.

Alex appeared to be coping actively in his endeavors, but the activity served as a defense against underlying passivity, symptoms of which, to name a few, were bouts of depression, suicidal ideation, and the projection of parts of his personality onto other members of his firm. "Splitting" is the psychological term to describe the disavowal of part of one's personality. We can all think of individuals in movies or in our work lives with "split" personalities—energetic, professional, and high achieving by day, addicts by night.

Alex had a split personality. He had not integrated traumatic experiences during childhood into his adolescent and adult personality, resulting in a coping style that was active on the surface but passive on less consciously controlled levels of personality. He enacted his split in his work relations at the venture capital firm, pitting one fund against the other, ultimately literally splitting the firm into two. The original firm dissolved, and two firms emerged, with Alex leading his group, which he relocated to a new state. That successor firm remains in business, but every partner except Alex left the firm within two years.

Alex is an example of an executive who thrived in those crisis situations in which he could act as an autonomous agent, bringing his aggression and business acumen to bear in troubleshooting and restoring failing businesses to profitability. He could not function in a partnership, nor could he build and lead a team, despite his cognitive understanding of team building as an essential leadership competency.

Developmental and Current-State Models

Psychologists make use of two complementary types of models—developmental and current state—to understand how and why humans behave in a specific way at a given stage of development. As the distinction between the two is essential to understanding my model, let me explain them in further detail.

Just as trait-based models focus on a specific set of traits, current-state models focus on a single event. This focus permits fine-grained analyses of cognitive processes that contribute to effective decisions. These models, however, are not designed to predict functioning over the long term; they may predict how individuals may behave in a similar situation within a month or even a year, but situations change, and human beings change. We learn, we grow, and, as we age, our mental and physical states change.

Developmental models are specifically designed to study this growth over extended periods of time, in much the same way that structural models consider the personality as a whole rather than looking at personality as an amalgamation of traits. You may have heard of research that involved tracking a group of children into adulthood to reveal how factors in their youth influenced their adult behavior.[2] These days, with our aging baby boomer population, many studies focus on changes brought on by aging and on why some seniors deteriorate and others thrive. These are examples of research based on developmental models. When applied to the study of leadership, developmental models can explain the protean qualities of effective leaders, their psychological resiliency and capacity to cope creatively with change—and their ability to encourage the expression of those qualities in others—or their potential to decline.

When selecting leaders, one must ask and answer a crucial question: "Does this person have the capacity to grow into the role?" Using short-term methods of assessment, there is generally no valid way to know whether a candidate who is right for the job now will still fit the position in later years as it evolves or will develop additional capabilities that the role may require in the future. In the case of high-level executives, the future demands of the role may be particularly elusive.

For this reason, I believe developmental models are underused in executive selection and deserving of more investigation. Current-state models are already in common usage by specialists in human resources and others responsible for screening job candidates. Developmental and current-state models are complementary, and both are necessary for a comprehensive and balanced account of human nature.

Three Illustrative Stories

Before discussing any executive as an exemplar of an active or passive coper or, as chapter 3 will discuss, as having a hole in his or her coping structure, I make the usual disclaimer: By tracing the precursors and manifestations of any executive's expressions of coping, I do not attempt to account for all aspects of his or her complex personality. In telling the stories I tell in this book, I limit myself to tracing the threads of the major preoccupations and dilemmas of competitive men and women as they ascend in their careers.

The stories below are drawn from assessments I performed on high-level executives in the running to become CEO. They illustrate successful predictions of three types: a correct identification of a capable leader, a warning to avoid an incapable leader, and advice to a board of directors on how to support a leader who was capable but missing some critical coping skills.

The first story illustrates an accurate prediction that the executive would succeed in a role with which he had no prior experience. When I assessed Wayne, he was serving as COO of a company undergoing a change of ownership from one equity sponsor to another. He had said he would leave the company if the new investors did not promote him to CEO when ownership changed.

Although Wayne had been an effective COO, he had never before been CEO and was relatively young to be placed in that role. The investors wanted to know whether he had the qualities to perform successfully as the CEO of a company that planned to grow internationally. They wanted to be aware of any significant issues with respect to his leadership and management skills. Could he establish himself as the CEO, a major strategist and the executive driving operational change and growth? His responsibilities would differ widely from those he had had as its COO. He would have to develop the strategy to foster international growth, build a strong management team aligned with that strategy, and grow the company both organically and through acquisitions, nationally and internationally, negotiating with prospective sellers and winning new customers.

The following summarizes my report to investors:

Wayne's performance on the various measures of cognitive ability indicates that he is extremely intelligent. He is a logical, sequential, and quick thinker. He has a sophisticated ability to think through alternative scenarios and synthesize a meaningful whole out of disparate pieces of information. He has the wisdom to accept his mistakes and learn from them.

Wayne also has social intelligence. His style encourages constructive conflict as a way to explore opportunities and resolve problems. He solicits the viewpoints of others before making final decisions. His readiness to perceive and integrate internal and external sources of information should allow him not only to formulate effective business strategy but also to motivate and work well with others in executing it.

Wayne's management style rests on a belief that his personal values apply as much to subordinates as they do to him. He sees himself as a father figure. He does not tolerate mediocrity or dishonesty. He requires integrity, reliability, and competent performance from his team and models these traits with his own behavior. He cultivates the support of his team while clearly seeking out the responsibilities as leader.

One of the few weaknesses in Wayne's functioning is that he becomes defensive when he fears that others have judged him as having done something bad. His need that others perceive him in a good light makes him slightly rigid and less open and creative than he could be. It also makes him dependent on superiors for recognition and praise.

Wayne possesses the emotional resources to cope with the demands of the CEO role, both now and in the future. He is extremely ambitious and believes he is now at a point in his career where he is ready to run an organization. I agree. Wayne has no noteworthy deficits in his leadership. Indeed, he is more than eager to demonstrate his capacities to lead.

To that end, I had one set of recommendations:

> Investors should be as explicit as possible with Wayne regarding expectations, goals, timetables, and resources he will have available (now and in the future). Because he is so conscientious, he tends not to respond well to what he perceives as vague and poorly defined expectations. Investors should couch their criticisms to minimize the chances that he feels perceived as a bad person. He might like financial rewards but would also like others to see his skills and ability to grow the business. Investors should give him appropriate feedback if things are going well and encourage him to keep up the good work.

Though Wayne had never been a CEO and had no past performance to demonstrate his abilities as chief executive, the assessment indicated he would be able to fulfill that position capably. I described Wayne as a conscientious and pragmatic executive focused on the bottom line. I predicted that he would do what it took to help the company be successful, achieving expectations in a moral way. This is exactly what he did. Upon exit, his investors earned a return of 3.3 times their invested capital.

The potential weakness I pointed out was that Wayne was sensitive to criticism and did not want to make a mistake. Investors related this tendency to the observation that he could have been quicker to terminate a manager who came along with an acquisition. "[Wayne] is conservative and doesn't have a quick trigger finger and will make sure it's the guy who can't succeed as opposed to the position. Ultimately we let him do what he thought was best."

In response to investors' questions about his potential to grow into the CEO role, the assessment answered with a definite "Yes!" His coping across situations over time and across levels of behavior was consistently active; he demonstrated unwavering integrity, and he was very successful as CEO.

Two years later, the investors sold the company Wayne ran. They rated him as an "outstanding" CEO who came in ahead of budget every single month they owned the company. Investors attributed the success of the investment to two factors. The first was the economic cycle: "The wind was not just at our back; it was howling at our back!" But they rated Wayne's leadership as a crucial factor in making the company successful.

The next executive, David, was the CEO of a startup planning to exploit buyout opportunities in a rapidly consolidating but still highly fragmented distribution industry. His story illustrates a failure of someone put into a CEO role. He had been a successful, smart corporate lawyer specializing in mergers and acquisitions and with credentials from a leading law school. On paper, he had the industry knowledge and technical skills that could lead his venture to success.

David's startup enjoyed no important advantages in terms of technology or marketing. The strategy was to identify good targets and to close acquisitions at attractive prices. The competition was fierce because several of the industry's global players were pursuing the same strategy. Management capability was therefore crucial, and David was part of a management team with formidable strengths.

David's responsibilities as CEO, however, would go significantly beyond what he had been doing as a corporate lawyer. A deal lawyer like David typically has relatively little to do with the decision to go after the deal in the first place or with how the new acquisition is managed after the deal closes. Even in the intervening space, the lawyer remains an agent who keeps his client well informed; he advises the client on both business and legal issues but ultimately leaves major decisions to the client. In his new position as CEO, David expected to make final decisions himself—he was now the client, so to speak, not the agent. It is not clear that either the investors or David had been fully aware of the problems this could pose. There were two problems. One, was he up to making the major decisions and seeing them through? And two, he expected to run the show himself and did not accept the guidance of the board or react well when given clear guidance.

Investors had already agreed to supply David's company with acquisition capital when they asked me to assess him. They cited doubts about his leadership of this business given his past experience. Did he possess the core leadership qualities needed as CEO to make the new venture successful? Their idea was partly to have David report to the board much more than he had expected to have to do. His responsibilities had changed, but his authority would be restricted until he convinced the investors that he was really able to deal with the challenges facing the company.

Here is what I recommended to his investors:

> David has a narrow expertise, and beyond this range—operating within a clear structure, in an autonomous fashion, following the legal code—his coping breaks down. If his company were to run into difficulty—if deadlines, timetables, or forecasts were missed—his passive coping would interfere with the venture being as successful as it needs to be.

Here is what the assessment showed:

> David is hard working, self-reliant, and verbally very intelligent. Yet his coping style is actually reactive and avoidant. He

is especially weak when working with others. He is not good at generating goals or overcoming obstacles. He does not easily tolerate ambiguity; the more poorly defined the problem, the more passive his coping.

David becomes extremely anxious when confronted by matters that require him to take initiative, improvise, or be decisive. At such times, he is unable to withstand the tension that would accompany seeking a full understanding of issues and working to resolve them. In an effort to get rid of problems that vex him, he offers facile, simplistic solutions that gloss over crucial details. As a result, he forecloses options when he would be better off reflecting more deeply and developing effective solutions.

This kind of passive coping compromises the quality of his judgment to such a degree that he would put his business at risk. Unfortunately, the issues most likely to make his business successful—such as finding targets at attractive prices and handling them in a timely manner—are precisely the issues likely to bring out his passive coping.

As investors worked more closely with David, they saw his weaknesses in collaborating with others that my assessment had highlighted. He negotiated a deal with a potential seller that specifically contravened investors' directives. (At that point in my work, I was not focused on integrity, but my subsequent review of his case and others made me keenly aware of its importance.) This and other behaviors, which were predicted in the assessment, caused them to put on the brakes by stopping providing new capital to the firm. They were eventually replaced by another private equity firm, but that firm saw his weaknesses and fired him. To my knowledge, David went back to his previous line of work as a lawyer.

My third story is about a CEO recruited to lead a business that had been family owned. The family members were seeking to sell to outside investors and to exit day-to-day management.

The investors identified as a candidate Mack, a twenty-five-year industry veteran, and asked me to assess him before making him CEO. Their primary question was whether Mack had the leadership, industry knowledge, and capability to run the business. They wanted a thorough assessment of how he would work with the existing management given that he would be part of a program of organizational change.

Here is what I reported to investors:

Mack has strong industry background and a history of turning around underperforming businesses. He is strongly motivated to achieve and succeed in a CEO role. He is honest and reliable. He is demanding, hard working, and has high standards.

Cognitively, Mack approaches the world in simple, black-and-white terms. Ambiguity and nuance are invisible to him. His way of seeing the world does not allow for creativity. His implementation is mechanical and without intuition.

Mack tends to shut out important human feelings such as compassion, which, in many cases, might generate more effective leadership. His style is rigid. He expects subordinates to execute in a logical, let's-do-it manner. If others resist, he assumes they are wrong and will not compromise.

What allows Mack to succeed is that he is intensely driven and self-confident. An excellent implementer, he will need close oversight from the company's directors to review and monitor his proposed plans. Conceiving strategies and understanding trends are not Mack's strengths, and his directors will have to help him.

To the extent Mack's managerial reforms represent much-needed medicine, he does nothing to make it taste better or go down smoother. This is not to say that his style will be unsuccessful. The situation requires meticulous execution and clear-cut direction of the workforce. The board of directors must supply the creativity and strategy as well as develop backchannel methods for staying attuned to the impact of Mack's changes on the corporate culture. Mack is not a perfect fit, but he is capable of doing what the organization requires.

Based on the assessment, I made two central recommendations:

One, Mack operates best within a chain of command. He sees the board as his superior. He expects the board to give him clear directives he can implement, which he then imposes on his subordinates. The board will need to devise corporate strategy without Mack's meaningful participation. He will not regard board members as advisors to consult or use them as a sounding board to debate important matters of policy. Once he understands a strategy, however, he will work hard to implement it.

Two, the board needs to involve itself in any matter involving the softer side of corporate culture because Mack is neither interested nor capable. The board will need to develop relations deeper within the organization to keep tabs on how the organization accepts or rejects the changes Mack implements.

To the extent his responsibilities are within his circle of competence, Mack is likely to be successful. He will do virtually anything to deliver on his commitments. Critical thinking and exercising nuanced judgments to exploit opportunities are not Mack's strengths, and the board will have to assume these responsibilities.

Mack's deficiencies as a leader were not insurmountable, and his style proved to be effective in a turnaround situation. Heeding my advice, investors gave him strategy in bite-size pieces that he could implement, which led the company to success. Overall, Mack had an active coping style coupled with a view of others as objects, not individuals. The investors, made aware of this, also stayed attuned to the effects of his hard-charging style on the culture of the company, stepping in to communicate changes to the organization in a manner the organization could accept.

As CEO, Mack quickly identified several areas for operational improvement, cost savings, and revenue enhancement. Investors used my assessment to create a support structure for Mack. His implementation of an aggressive strategic plan yielded positive results, as forecasted. Four years later when the industry recovered, the company emerged with market-leading positions, low-cost manufacturing, a lean organization, and a talented and aggressive sales team. Outstanding, focused execution by Mack had resulted in the company's becoming an attractive platform from which to build a national competitor as opposed to a regional one. The company was sold to a financial sponsor, generating superior returns to investors. They called it a "home run," having earned a return of 4.4 times their invested capital.

If the board had not known what they could and could not expect from Mack, they might not have been so fortunate. Had they relied on Mack for strategic thinking or the softer sides of corporate culture, they might not have generated the returns they did. But the psychological assessment gave them an understanding of his psychological and management strengths and blind spots. That awareness helped them monitor Mack's performance through backchannels in order to mitigate the impact of the changes he implemented on the organization's culture, making the changes more acceptable and to generate a successful result.

Predictions Made and Missed

As the three examples above show, I do not rely on a model that seeks to explain a wide variety of situations in general, one-size-fits-all terms. I do not seek to establish the average effect of one powerful variable on a large set of companies. Instead, I seek to tailor-make a fit. I try to understand how executives achieve success; the complexities of interactions among person, organization, and the outer world; and to optimize the precision of my predictions over time.[3] It is my belief that investors, board members, and executives can reduce their risk across many individual, possibly unique situations by assessing the candidates and the environment, current and potential future, in which they are expected to perform.

As is also clear from these examples, the predictions themselves become part of the process. I explain the findings of my assessment to investors or board members and to the candidate who is ultimately chosen. The findings sometimes change the behavior of both parties. I also assess the impact of my conclusions during this process. If investors follow my advice, as in the case of Mack, they may be able to alter the degree of their executives' success or failure. The model, then, participates in the dynamics that it predicts.

Let me stress that the predictive validity of the assessments is not 100 percent. Early on, I was too tough in evaluating one CEO on the quality of his strategic vision though overall I strongly recommended him for the position. His investors challenged my assessment of his strategic vision, and in subsequent years their judgment turned out to be right. Following up on whether an assessment indicator is accurate—or to what extent it is not—helps me refine my model and improve the accuracy of future assessments.

In two other assessments I missed the potential for the CEOs to engage in sexual behavior that could have harmed my clients' reputations and cost them money. In one case, the client was in the midst of selling the company when a person reporting directly to the CEO filed a sexual harassment lawsuit against the CEO. In the other case, a CEO, whom investors trusted to make the right choice, recommended a personal friend to replace him as he sought retirement. Phone records later showed that the new CEO spent large parts of his paying day working on matters not related to running the company. It also became well known among the workers at the company that he had numerous sexual affairs. No one blew the whistle; his COO and CFO effectively ran the company. He was immediately terminated when, six months into the investment, during the investors' first on-site visit, they walked in on him in a bar and saw him in thoroughly inappropriate female company. Very shortly thereafter, they investigated his computer and cellphone records, which verified that he had put in very little time attending to the company's business.

The latter two mistakes led me to make an in-depth study of integrity in business executives. Integrity, one of the four elements of active coping, was already a part of my model, but I have come to put more emphasis on its importance in predicting effective performance. Without integrity, the strengths of the other elements cannot be consistently directed for the long-term good of the executive or the organization. I consider integrity in more depth in chapter 5.

All models are probabilistic: Whether potential strengths and weaknesses materialize depends on a number of factors, including environmental circumstances that may emerge over time. A properly trained clinical psychologist can identify potential psychological risk factors identified by using projective techniques, a topic I will take up in the next chapter. No candidate is perfect. A good assessment can help a board of directors identify the candidate who may not meet all the criteria for success in the role yet may be the better candidate. I recently assessed a young candidate (age thirty-nine) for CEO. His expertise was narrow, deep, and highly sophisticated but without much leadership experience, particularly with the types of challenges the company would face in the future. The alternative was a candidate who had strong credentials as a successful leader from within the same industry as the client company. His leadership style, however, was not a fit for the client company, and he was significantly less intelligent than the younger, less experienced candidate. Through the heavy-handed persuasion of two members of the board of directors, they were able to turn to the first candidate. The board and I believed the candidate would grow into the role as CEO, and he did.

In addition, given that no candidate is perfect, the assessment (and board of directors) should identify where the finalist falls short and determine how to help him or her overcome the areas of shortcoming. Directors need to discuss openly the risks they take when choosing that candidate. They should try to envision how that candidate might develop over time. Because my assessment approach is developmental in nature, it can aid considerably in advising boards on this aspect of future development. Many boards have adopted the practice of appointing an experienced director (or the former CEO in the case I just noted above) to mentor and coach the new CEO through his or her first year, to help the new CEO succeed.

Some predictions may take time to materialize, and luck, good or bad, is always a factor. Prediction at best can be only probable, not certain. Circumstances surrounding companies generally change over time, frequently in ways that are hard to predict. Board members and investors cannot rely on static models that assume circumstantial stability.[4] It is a central theme of my work to develop strategies to address this uncertainty.

3

Coping Styles and Coping Holes

AS NOTED EARLIER, active coping contributes to healthy personality growth and strong performance. It does this by optimizing an individual's responses to specific problems and by fostering continuing psychological richness, self-confidence, and resourcefulness. Success and, as we will see in the story of Tim later in this chapter, even failure create a base of experience on which future coping is built. Active copers are not free of all personality flaws, but they face internal obstacles with the same courage and forward momentum with which they face external challenges.

Passive copers have characteristic tactics they favor. Sometimes those are useful tactics, but possessing a limited repertoire of responses is unlikely to cover all the necessary situations. Some passive copers, like David, the first CEO described in chapter 2, may give in to their fears without fully considering the consequences: they impulsively follow their emotions. When stressed, they make decisions very quickly. But the rapidity of their decisions owes less to confidence in their judgment than to a desire to escape the tensions caused by the problem. Their actions are designed to make them feel better now as opposed to dealing with the situation.

Other passive copers consistently behave in accord with outside pressures; they depend on external instructions and guidelines and maintain a status quo. In the long run, active copers, because they can alter their tactics to fit the specific demands of situations, have a higher probability of success than passive copers, who must rigidly comply with internal and/or external compulsions. Familiar signs of passive coping include dithering, retreating into minutiae, paralysis in the face of major threats, uncharacteristic outbursts of rage, and over-control of others.

Two Stories of Active Coping

Tim

Take Tim, the founder and CEO of a provider of management systems for oncology specialists. The morning I first met with him, he and his team had just completed a new public offering. His board had urged this action to help finance the longer-term growth of the company and was very supportive of Tim for having taken it. Tim's anxiety was palpable. Out spilled his concerns. On this day, he told me, he felt even more insecure than he had when he first took the company public. He spontaneously traced his anxieties back to tensions he had picked up as a child from his parents' strained relationship.

Tim grew up in the rural heartland. He described his father as a dreamer who did not act on his entrepreneurial instincts and ambitions. His mother was cautious and fearful that her husband's dreams would destroy their economic security. Their marriage was tense. Tim's mother inhibited his father, who complied with her wishes that he stick to a "safe" position that offered limited opportunities for advancement and personal growth. Tim's father would say, "You can do whatever you want, son," but he didn't do what *he* wanted. He gave in to his wife, held himself back, and was steadily but unhappily employed.

Tim internalized two different messages about achievement from his mother and father. His mother was frightened by lofty ambition; his father was a frustrated dreamer. Tim's father transferred his ambitions to his son, who was clearly susceptible: Tim was energetic, determined, and intellectually brilliant. He believed that he could achieve whatever he set out to do. But he also believed that if he pursued his ambitions, his mother's fears would come true.

To deal with the conflicting messages he got from his parents, Tim downplayed his ambition—all the time secretly dreaming of ways to achieve. When Tim left home for college, he had a dilemma: should he strive to achieve or hold himself back? If he held back, he would renounce his passion and lose what could give his life meaning. If he did not hold back, he felt unprotected. Rather than cope actively with the conflict, he partied. He flunked out of college his junior year and returned home to work as a delivery truck driver. This job brought him into contact with individuals across a wide socioeconomic spectrum. Tim saw that he could do more in life than drive a truck. He began to dream again. This time, he resolved he would achieve. He completed college, earned a master's degree in engineering, and started to apply his engineering training to innovations in cancer care.

Tim made the decision to achieve despite his anxieties. Although his achievement has been a laborious and painful process, he made the choice to pursue his ambitions rather than yield to his fears. Tim's conscious managing of his weakness is an example of active coping. He experienced a dilemma, confronted the tradeoffs, and made a choice to pursue his passion knowing well the anxieties he felt and would probably always feel. As an adult, he has the ability to transcend the anxieties of the moment, at least sufficiently to make a choice that gives him and his company the best chance of growth.

Scott

Individuals who possess active coping personality structures are masters of flexible response. For example, an executive I'll call Scott became CEO of a company facing disastrous debt. On an operating basis, however, the company had been performing exceptionally well. It also had outstanding employees who were proud of their accomplishments. Scott decided to reorganize the company by putting it into chapter 11 bankruptcy long before others thought it was necessary. He made this decision even though at that time any decision to take a company into bankruptcy was viewed in the business community with disdain. He made the decision to avoid further deterioration of the company's debt-related financial position. Employees were shocked and dismayed.

Scott's decision allowed him to restructure the company within the year, repay all of the creditors in full, and initiate a new-product growth program. It led to a very successful outcome. Scott knew his decision would initially be regarded as highly questionable and put his credibility at risk. He said, in retrospect, "Sometimes the vision can only be seen by you, yet you have to have the courage to proceed with it despite how it is read. This is probably the most difficult business decision I have ever made."

Scott is a shining example of an active coper who, despite the pressures of his management team, his board, and the capital markets, made an effective decision and acted on it. Active copers are usually effective but, as discussed earlier, are not always successful. In this case Scott was both—demonstrating the flexibility an active coping style affords in response to challenging situations. Scott was a leader who had the good fortune to be successful.

One Story of Passive Coping

Ernest Hemingway is an example of a man with an underlying structural basis of passivity that emerged in later life. Ernest's mother had six children with her husband, whom she regarded as inadequate, both sexually and as a provider, and who did the cooking at home.[1] His mother saw Ernest as the child most like her and treated him as a boy as if he were her twin. She treated his sister, the eldest child, as if they were of the same gender: at times, she dressed them as little girls of the age, at times, as boys. (Both ultimately committed suicide, as their father also would.)

Outside the home, Ernest's father was a respected doctor and an accomplished hunter and fisherman, skills he passed to his son. Ernest's childhood development taught him that a man's masculinity was constantly in jeopardy within the home. But outside the home, it could be preserved and even enhanced by courageous acts, contests with nature, and competing with other men.

Ernest left home as soon as he could. In 1918, before he finished high school, he enlisted with the World War I ambulance drivers. He was seriously wounded by mortar fire in July of that year and was forced to return home. He completed high school and in 1921 married the first of four wives. Marriage and the couple's subsequent move to Paris where he worked as a war correspondent kept him at a safe psychological distance from his mother. Ernest was famous for his machismo image. His third wife, also a foreign war correspondent, saw through his manly façade shortly after their honeymoon. She scoffed at him and ultimately rejected him, a painful insult to his sense of manliness. As he aged, having suffered multiple, severe injuries throughout his adult years (too numerable to list here), his problems projecting a masculine image appeared. As his literary friends began dying, he became increasingly depressed. During this period, he suffered from severe headaches, weight problems, diabetes, and high blood pressure, much of which resulted from his many previous accidents and many years of heavy drinking.[2] It has been argued that with the onset of aging he could no longer hide from the feminine identifications within his psyche.[3] Symptomatically, he drank heavily, so much so that it interfered with his thinking, and he developed paranoia and the depression that ultimately led to his suicide at age sixty-one.

Interestingly, Hemingway began writing his last novel, *The Garden of Eden*, at age forty-six, shortly after his third wife's insulting rejection of him was finalized in divorce. He completed it at age sixty-one. (It was published posthumously.) The work seems to have been an attempt to sublimate his inner preoccupations through art. It tells the tale of a wife (like his mother) who transforms into a masculine figure and tries to demolish her husband's masculinity. In that sense, the novel is about the temptations and threats of androgyny, stemming back to his mother's treatment of him and the other male in the household, his father. Ernest Hemingway is a clear example of a passive coper.

An Active Coper with a Hole

As the following story of Sam illustrates, lying may be a sign of a hole in the coping structure of an otherwise active coping individual. Once again, I make the disclaimer that I do not try to account for most elements of his complex personality. In telling Sam's tale, I describe an executive with an otherwise robust personality structure that had a hole in its coping.

Sam had been extremely successful in his career as an executive in the semiconductor industry. At age fifty, he was brought in as a partner in a venture capital firm. Everything he had told about his career suggested he was a straight shooter, but my client had done very poor due diligence on this important hire. I did not assess Sam. Once he joined the firm, his partners noticed that he told brazen lies.[4] When he entertained the firm's limited partners, he lied about the size of his boat and his share of ownership of a jet. (His wife confirmed that his lying about the size of his possessions was typical of Sam.) His partners stopped taking him on golf outings with clients because he would do things like move his ball or kick it when it was behind a tree. He did not count some of his strokes. In "improving the lie," he lied about his golf score.

Sam's lying seemed to make everyone but Sam uncomfortable. It compromised his record of actually making fairly good investment decisions. There was a sense among his partners that if he lied about his golf score, he would lie about more important matters. They did not believe his reports on existing or prospective deals. They suspected him of omitting information that was material for sound decisions. By lying about something utterly trivial, Sam raised doubts about everything he said. His partners did not want to trust him with important aspects of being a partner and found a way to oust him.

What would cause an ambitious man like Sam to tell easily checkable lies that could sabotage his career? There are liars who are so glib, so experienced, so natural in their lying that few people suspect them and fewer still bother to check. Sam had a hole in his coping structure. Sam's lying was the kind of behavior unlikely to be identified by conventional techniques. He was a con man, a salesman, skilled at telling convincing lies. When learning about Sam's relationship to his demanding father and his father's inability to accept Sam as less intelligent than he, I could at least infer one source of his insecurities—and proclivity to lie to cover them when in the presence of those he considered superior to him.

Sam did not deal effectively with his needs for self-esteem. Despite his prior accomplishments, he felt (in view of his father's failure to accept his abilities for what they were) he was a fraud. His career success as a semiconductor executive should have disproved his underlying belief that he was inferior. But when that success was put side by side with that of successful venture capitalists, Sam's sense of inferiority overwhelmed his judgment.

In an entirely new situation for Sam, in which his peers' success and intelligence (I did assess most of the other members of the partnership) exceeded his own, he coped passively.

Sam's lying functioned psychologically to boost his self-esteem by compensating for the inferiority he felt. Some might consider beefing up the size of their possessions to be an exaggeration to get ahead in business. Sam did. He thought he would gain respect—but did not fully think through the consequences of his lies. Instead, he wrecked his reputation in the VC community. A healthier executive with Sam's ambition would have found ways to bolster his confidence without engaging in career-limiting behavior.

Winston Churchill may be another example of an active coper with a coping hole. He was a great leader of a nation during World War II and generally a successful politician. His hole was the "black dog" of depression that he struggled against much of his life.[5] Usually, he was able to pull himself out of it.

I have never heard or read a formal definition of the term "coping hole." One needs the concept of a coping hole to account for occasional "breakdowns" or inconsistencies in a given individual's functioning. Sometimes these inconsistencies may result from unusual external circumstances (such as a debilitating illness or significant personal losses), but often they stem from internal weaknesses.

Holes, as Jordan Jacobowitz and I have discussed them, differ from structural configurations. Structural configurations are more systemic and diffuse throughout the personality system and when manifest affect general functioning. Take Ernest Hemingway. Holes are certain "sore" spots and can occur on any level of psychological functioning. For example, an individual may be an active coper characteristically but under prolonged stress or in certain types of situations, when faced with solving a problem alone, may experience certain anxieties or depressive reactions resulting in circumscribed maladaptive behaviors. Take Sherlock Holmes's use of cocaine or Freud's fainting spells or Clinton's extracurricular sex activities. Holes are imperfections in an otherwise sturdy structure. Churchill struggled with depression but was otherwise extremely successful.

It is possible that holes and structural configurations can interact, such that when the passive side of the personality manifests, it manifests first in the area where holes already exist. In the case of a man like Hemingway, rejection by a wife induced his repressed weak, conflicted side, setting off a downhill trajectory.

Sam's lying indicated a hole in his self-esteem. He generally functioned well but could not tolerate being seen in an inferior light, for whatever reason, and needed to protect that "sore" point. When feeling secure, or in most situations that did not tap into either his self-esteem or perhaps something to do with his sense of uncorrupted masculinity, he coped actively, but when his sense of adequacy seemed threatened (particularly in certain competitive situations), he lied to maintain inner security.

The next chapter explains how psychologists assess personality systemically, in terms of levels of behavior ranging from conscious to unconscious, their degree of congruence, and the implications of the degree of congruence among them for predicting an executive's long-term performance.

4

What Lies Beneath?

Everyone then who hears these words of mine and does them
will be like a wise man who built his house on the rock.

— MATTHEW 7:24

Sorting the False from the Positive

In business, we tend to see mainly the public, external façade.
Books about business leaders rarely discuss the significance of
executives' inner lives and the effects that early development and
unconscious aspects of decision making—the full and complex
structure of character and personality—have on performance at
work. Most candidates regard as intrusive anything more than a
rather limited examination of their private sides. Although privacy
is to be respected, most people would acknowledge that executives' inner lives can and do affect their decisions at work. Executives who are at home with who they are as human beings will
be successful much more often than those who are not. Mental
health, which includes active coping, is enormously important for
lasting effectiveness as an executive.

Understanding the whole person, public and private, exterior
and interior, past and present, makes it possible to develop better
predictions regarding an executive's performance at work. As the

contrast between Sam and Tim showed, knowing the whole person one can see how the expectations of a father fostered a set of ambitions in his son, how the parents' relationship led their son to develop a particular personality style, and how those elements blended to form the meaning the adult son gives to work. Knowing the whole person means looking beyond how the person appears at a purely outward-facing professional level. As noted repeatedly, a person's sense of happiness, contentment, or success comes from the merger of personal and professional aspects (including family dynamics such as a relationship with a spouse or a parent) with the person's early history, which helps one understand the whole person.

Chapter 1 told four stories, two about active copers, one about a passive coper, and one about an otherwise active coper with a "hole" in his coping that indicated shortcomings in integrity. Chapter 4 is an attempt to explain how my assessment process allows one to differentiate among active and passive copers, how to pinpoint where they may be weak or strong, and to understand the nature of their particular leadership styles. It is technical in nature but does not discuss the particular data collection instruments in detail. Table 4.1 details the areas that can bear on an executive's performance and that I consider as part of my assessment.

Self-Report Methods

Executives disclose only a limited amount of information about themselves in interviews or questionnaires. These standard hiring tools are relatively structured and permit canned or rehearsed responses. The questions are obvious, transparent, and easily manipulated. Most executives know what to conceal and what to reveal—about themselves, their experience, and the depth of

Table 4.1
Factors in Executive Performance

Business culture	Environment in which the executive is expected to perform, including competitive strategy, industry dynamics, culture of the organization, management team, and exit strategy
Intelligence, work skills, and experience	Generally revealed on resumes, during interviews, and through reference checks and psychometric testing (the latter for work style and cognitive ability)
Development	Past development (which helps us to articulate motivation and capabilities) and current development needs (possible midlife concerns, thoughts of retirement)
Personal life areas	Nonbusiness aspects of life that can affect performance at work such as family, leisure, religious beliefs, and sustaining social relationships
Personality structure and dynamics	Different levels and functions of personality both conscious and unconscious, including motives, coping, interpersonal style, and integrity

their commitment. They will reveal—indeed, they will highlight—what makes them look good and conceal what does not. We call this "faking good." Everyone considered to lead a company looks good on paper.

Résumés, CVs, interviews, most common human resources tests, and reference checks are called "overt" or "self-reporting."

Job candidates have full control over the data they include (and exclude) and can present the best image of themselves. In a job interview, executives may put a spin on the stories they tell, claiming to be persistent and hard working when what they really are is stubborn. That is a classic example of faking good. Even the most astute interviewer will have trouble distinguishing perseverance from stubbornness.

Projective Techniques

Self-report methods have their place in the assessment and hiring process. I conduct interviews, read résumés, and use my own questionnaires. But I also use projective techniques. Projective techniques provide little structure to guide the response, giving candidates few to no cues for how to control the image they project of themselves. The ambiguity of the stimulus requires them to pull an unscripted response spontaneously from within themselves. Because they are not consciously aware of the deeper aspects of psychological functioning elicited by the projective techniques, they cannot fake good. Projective measures reveal aspects of psychological functioning that are inaccessible when using objective techniques, such as what others say about a person. (Refer to appendix B for a detailed description of the assessment process, including the projective data collection instruments.)

A sentence completion test is one example of a semiprojective technique. It is a test I administer on the spot to elicit a series of responses, each item of which provides a partial structure that must be completed spontaneously by the candidate. Even executives who claim to be no-nonsense, take-charge leaders may find it difficult—if not impossible—to complete certain sentence stems. For example, "When he failed in his work . . . " To complete the stem, the subject must mobilize energy, orient attention, and commit to make a response. He can respond actively, passively, or not at all.

The most powerful projective technique that I use to assess leaders is a storytelling test. It uses a set of pictures, about each of which the candidate must tell a story evoked by the picture. The pictures were designed to elicit paradigmatic themes in human development. Those I have selected to use are particularly relevant to leadership situations.[1] The storytelling projective technique enables a psychologist to pull together various aspects collected via the other assessment techniques and connect them with motives, coping, interpersonal relatedness, degree of optimism, and outcomes.

The best understanding of the total structure of personality is achieved when we take into account the overt behavior in conjunction with the covert tendencies expressed on the projective storytelling technique. Comparing responses across conscious, semiconscious, and unconsciously controlled communication about the self makes it possible to begin to make inferences about the degree of congruence or conflict in coping, motivation, and interpersonal style.

Research conducted with my colleague Jordan Jacobowitz in 2004 used the storytelling projective technique to assess CEOs identified by their investors as "successful."[2] We found a range of patterns, from CEOs who were psychologically organized in a secure, resilient, and self-satisfied way to those who revealed underlying areas of defensiveness and vulnerability. Evidence shows that CEOs with the latter pattern are more limited in their abilities to lead in a consistent and effective manner. Depending on the specific profile, individuals in this latter group may falter in completing their objectives if they encounter disrupting changes, either at work or at home.

Let's compare two sets of successful CEOs who participated in the study mentioned in the previous paragraph and the characteristics revealed by an interpretation of three of their stories. The first CEO is Steve. The first story he created was in response to a picture of a young boy contemplating a violin that rests on a table before him." Steve's story was as follows:

> Here's [he gave his own first name] at his early age in elementary school, studying and dreaming about what the future holds. As he looks back, he has fond memories of friendships that he enjoyed and is appreciative of the efforts everyone made to bring him to where he is today.

The character or hero (with whom the storyteller identifies and has injected into the story he creates) is successful and looks back upon his childhood friendships and relationships that helped him achieve success. The outcome is the success of the hero, who appreciates the supportive efforts of others in his path to achievement. Feelings toward others are "fond" and appreciative. The storyteller integrates past, present, and future in a logical, efficient, coherent manner.

The second card I give presents a country scene: a young woman holding books stands in the foreground, a man is plowing the fields, and an older woman is looking on while standing in the background. In response to this picture, this CEO told the following story:

> This is a story about the people and their relationships. . . .
> The family is working the fields, providing for themselves, expecting another child. The older daughter is going off to school. To me it communicates the bonds that everyone has and the roles that everyone plays supporting each other and it looks like a happy family, and for me the take away is the development of each person individually and yet as part of a family unit. This story highlights the theme of "one for all and all for one."

The next story was told in response to a picture of an unclothed man gripping a rope, which he may be climbing or sliding down. The expression on his face is ambiguous.

This is the story of a man who has the ability to climb up and down a rope. He found the dream opportunity performing in Cirque d' Soleil, and even though he's aging, he still performs today and feels a great sense of accomplishment that his body allows him to perform, and he's very satisfied with his role.

This story captures the CEO's sheer enjoyment of personal success and a pervasive sense of self-satisfaction.

Steve is an example of a CEO who has managed to blend his personal ambitions for success with social and familial values. The stories he tells in response to the pictures emphasize how characters recognize their interdependency upon others and how success is always a mutual enterprise, one balancing the needs of self and others. His stories demonstrate congruency among his self-reported achievements in life, motives, core values, and personal desires.

Another CEO, George, appeared just as content, resilient, and self-confident as Steve. To the picture of a boy contemplating the violin before him, he told the following story:

Bobby was a young boy who had to take violin. His mother and father believed that he should learn culture. Bobby wanted to play sports. He religiously played the violin to fulfill his one-hour-a-day practice requirements and even an occasional recital, but his true love was the tennis courts. Finally, after struggling for ten years to play the violin, he won his first tennis tournament and went on to become a great tennis player. He never did learn to really enjoy the violin.

George depicts Bobby as someone who keeps trying, knowing he has to fulfill his obligation and his parents' belief, but he also followed his heart, ultimately succeeded in fulfilling his desires, and achieved greatness in so doing.

To the picture of the man plowing the fields, a pregnant woman, and a young woman in the distance, George told the following story:

"Life on the Farm": a title. We lived on a farm in rural Kansas. As you can see my mother was pregnant. There were many children. We all had tasks to perform. It was our job to help raise the crops, tend to the livestock. It was all part of our upbringing, but it made it difficult to get a good education. Elizabeth wanted to be a student. She was a good student. She loved reading; she loved working with children, and she didn't care a lot about the farm. She also resented the life that her mother had because she had to work so hard for so many hours a day. Elizabeth wanted to be better than that, to have more, to tour more places than just rural Kansas. So she worked on the farm to scrimp up enough money to finally attend a university outside the state. She went on to become a world-renowned poet, Elizabeth Browning. And now you know the rest of the story.

In this story, George revealed the need to go beyond environmental limitations and reverse the fear of becoming overwhelmed by circumstance by transforming it into glorious success. This refusal to be overwhelmed by external forces and transformation into "glorious success" is an example of active coping.

Finally, George told this story to the man clinging to a rope:

Called "The Rope of Life." As you can see from the picture, life is represented by a rope and how to climb it. The higher you go, the more mental and physical strength it requires. When your feet are on the ground and you are holding onto the rope, it is kind of like childhood. You have something to hold on to, to hold you up, and to orient you, and you have a stable foundation. But as you rise, pull-by-pull, kick-by-kick, it gets a little tougher. Sometimes you slide backwards. It actually burns your hands. Sometimes you bleed it's so painful. But you know you can't go back to the ground, you have to move on, so you try a little harder, you think about ways to deal with the pain and the stress and you realize you can move forward and upward, you have to make time for those sacrifices. Sometimes you don't have time for eating, for sleeping. In the end, it is worth it, but don't let somebody tell you that you can let go of the rope; it's easier, because when you have hit the ground it hurts and you have to start over. So the moral of the story is: plan your next move, focus, hang on, deal with problems at hand, and in the end you'll achieve the heights of success.

In this story, George expresses his philosophy that perseverance and coping are the keys to success.

In contrast to Steve, George emphasized much more the personal needs of the stories' central characters and emphasized how success was tied to the perseverance and drive of the individual and not the collective support received from others. In fact, the message seemed to be that successful individuals must go beyond others' expectations and pursue their own goals relentlessly. One must respect others but not let their desires or limitations become insuperable impediments to success and self-actualization.

Steve's stories indicated that his leadership style would be communal. He would be best suited to a growth-oriented business in which employees need to be recognized for their positive contributions to the business and remain loyal employees. His integrity, intelligence, and active coping suggest that he would not tolerate fools, however, and put the reputation of the business or the loyalty of his virtuous employees at risk. George's stories indicated a charismatic, forceful, take-no-prisoners leadership style. His stories indicate that he would be best suited to turnarounds, work in which he in fact excelled over the bulk of his career.

Both Steve and George gave active coping stories. In contrast to George and Steve were two CEOs, Tom and Sandy, whose stories revealed covert tendencies toward passive coping *despite their similarities to George and Steve on the overt, conscious level.* For example, Tom told the following stories to the same three pictures reported in the first two sets of examples.

In response to the picture of a boy sitting before a violin, Tom told the following story:

> The little boy, we'll call him Timmy, has just been given a violin and he is trying to learn how to play. But he's pretty much decided he'll give it a chance.

That story—his entire story—is remarkably short. The main character does not possess an internal desire to play or achieve. His motivation is linked to accommodating himself to external impositions. There is no development of a plot, no other people are involved, feelings are missing, and there is no decisive end. The story lacks vitality.

Tom told the following story in response to the picture of two women and a man on a farm:

> The young woman has decided that or has been wondering whether or not she should stay home with the family in a traditional farm or should she go off and do something else and try and get an education, and since she is holding books, she is embracing an education; she will go off and do what she wants and forsake the family farm. She's sad about that, but she's decided it's the right thing to do.

In this story, the character is decisive in a way but is unable to blend her needs with the family she cares about. A sense of sadness and self-justification pervades the ending.

Tom told the following story in response to the picture of a man gripping a rope:

> The kid's in gym class. He just learned how to climb the rope. He's climbed the rope and he's happy about it.

This story, though happy sounding, demonstrates the simple way Tom views his world, avoiding perceiving or dealing with the potential stressors and intricacies of life.

Finally, Tom told this story in response to a picture of a young man with downcast head, eyes shielded by a forearm; behind him is the figure of a woman lying in bed, breasts exposed:

> The first thing that pops into my mind is that the woman is sick or in some other distress and the guy is distraught about it and doesn't know what to do; is beside himself with worry.

This story reveals the basic sense of helplessness beneath Tom's overt façade that may emerge at stressful times. The main character is paralyzed with worry and takes no action. There is no resolution.

Indeed, each of Tom's stories was riddled with passive coping tendencies. Each story revealed tendencies toward constriction, defensiveness, and uncertainty, *despite the fact that he consciously described himself as an active, open, energetic, and confident individual.* This contrast suggests that he attempts to ward off weakness or self-doubt and defensively proceeds as if these parts of him do not exist. He is at risk of encountering those split-off parts of his self when the internal and external means he uses to distance them are challenged and overwhelmed. And in fact, investors eventually dismissed Tom from his job on the grounds that he had ignored an ultimately successful unionizing attempt by workers. His failure to perceive—much less resolve—labor-management tensions forced his investors to oust him and bring in a CEO to turn the business around. His projective stories reveal in style and content the tendency to simplify complex situations, to avoid conflict, and to be passive before threatening situations. He fails to integrate social and personal motivations.

The stories of a fourth CEO, Sandy, who was also part of the study on successful CEOs, likewise reveal pervasive insecurities that lie beneath a self-presentation of confidence and success. In response to the picture of the boy in front of a violin, Sandy told this story:

> He's looking at the violin and wondering why he can't play it and is thinking about all the other things he could be doing if his parents didn't say he had to play the violin and he wished it came easy to him so he could go on to do those other things, which is what he will do shortly and be much happier. The end.

In response to the picture of the man on the farm and two women, Sandy told the following story:

> She is wondering about her future and is so deep in thought that she doesn't notice the strapping guy in the back or the Amish woman by the tree but she is deep in thought on a million things and then she trips and falls because she was deep in thought but then gets up again and continues on her way.

There is no depiction of a family unit. None of the characters are related to the others. The main character is so caught up in herself that she fails to take note of the others, even though the storyteller can identify them. This degree of solitary thought and failure to integrate others into the story stands in contrast to the story told by Steve, which he summarizes as the "development of each person individually and yet as part of a family unit" and to that told by George, which describes the compliance of the young woman with her obligations to her family and its business and her success in also fulfilling her personal goals.

And in response to the picture of the man gripping a rope, Sandy said:

> He read a brochure one day that challenged him to face his fears and he realized he was afraid of heights but given the introduction that he should face his fears, he decided to climb the rope nonetheless and when climbing the rope he found it was easier to be up high than he realized and he found that he enjoyed the view although he wished he had put some clothes on before climbing.

The characters in each of Sandy's stories feel pressured by others, struggle to remain on their feet, and are driven by their fears, and they find themselves "nakedly" embarrassed despite their efforts.[3]

These two pairs of contrasting sets of stories—George and Steve versus Tom and Sandy—show that although material from the developmental histories and objective tests may be very similar among senior executives, the projective stories indicate differences on the more private level of fantasy and inner life. These differences are important in making long-term predictions about the stability and course of coping, behavior, and leadership effectiveness.

Executives who demonstrate active coping in explicitly structured situations such as role-playing exercises may not manifest active coping at the deeper levels revealed by projective techniques. Projective techniques may expose them as passive copers. When the measures on different levels disagree, a red flag goes up. An executive may present himself as having all the qualities that make up active coping, but projective measures reveal he is anything but. Under stress, this discrepancy may well resolve itself in the direction of underlying passive tendencies, compromising decision making in real life. A strong building on a weak foundation crumbles.

Projective techniques like those described above get at underlying coping and motivation in ways that permit psychologists to make inferences about how the individual will function under greater stress. They tap into aspects of personality that most of us either do not know or do not want to reveal—desires, fears, and conflicts that we may disavow or repress.

Multilevel Typology

Harking back to the iceberg, its tip above the surface is the conscious level of functioning. It can be seen functioning in observable behavior. The semiconscious level is like the part of the iceberg just visible below the waterline. The unconscious level is the largest part of the iceberg, hidden in the mysterious depths.

Psychologists can test the coping strength of each of these levels separately. A high level of coping is rated H, a medium level is rated M, and a low level of coping is rated L. A rating of HHH, for example, means that the subject demonstrated high levels of coping across all three levels of awareness, the sign of a person with strong active coping. Someone with an LLL rating would invariably be passive. Most people fall somewhere between these two extremes. Any time there is a large discrepancy among coping on different levels (HHL, HML, and HLL), the rating indicates that the test subject has an unstable structure of coping. Think of this unstable structure as the house built upon sand, from the famous parable quoted at the beginning of this chapter: "Everyone then who hears these words of mine and does them will be like a wise man who built his house on the rock."

Unconscious coping forms the foundation for the conscious levels of coping—what we see of a person's behavior. A low level of unconscious coping provides a weak foundation (the sand), and a high level of unconscious coping provides a strong foundation (the rock). A person can control her conscious behavior to give

Table 4.2
Multilevel Coping Types

Assessment Technique	Level of Behavior	Coping Type		
Objective	Consciously controlled	High	High	High
Semiprojective	Semiconsciously controlled	High	High	Low
Projective	Unconsciously controlled	High	Low	Low
Type		HHH	HHL	HLL
Risk assessment		No risk	Some risk	High risk

the appearance of strength, but if her underlying coping is weak, the storms and stresses of life will crack and eventually tear down her coping structure.

As we age, our defenses weaken, and our underlying coping style comes to the fore. This effect can cause a noticeable change in behavior and personality. As previously discussed, Hemingway was famous for his façade of toughness and machismo, but his depression, paranoia, and suicide in later life indicate a weakness in his unconscious coping (related to concerns about androgyny). He epitomizes an HLL personality structure.

Conversely, some people may seem outwardly passive but have inner reserves of activity and strength. A tired, middle-aged black woman living in the South in 1955 who refused to move to the back of the bus may exemplify emergence in mid-life of hidden reserves of active coping. She may exemplify the LHH rating (although in that time and place, neither women nor African Americans were encouraged to be active copers). Hemingway reverted to what I call a passive stance and Rosa Parks to an active one.[4]

A high-stress situation can strip men and women of their defenses and force them to fall back to their unconscious style of coping. At times, this revelation can cause a change in conscious, overt personality, as the person in crisis is forced to confront or enact his or her underlying, covert coping strategies. (Think of Hemingway as an example of the stressors of aging on a man with systemic underlying passivity.) It may shake the confidence of an HLL type to discover he is not as strong as he thought, and this discovery may lead to an increase in the dominance of underlying passivity or trigger collapse. On the other hand, an outwardly passive person may gain self-assurance from coping well under pressure. Adults can grow and change for the better.

Some individuals have particular skills and supports that enable them to function well under some circumstances for some period of time. They appear to be active copers until they begin to falter. They are partial active copers with weaknesses that emerge under certain circumstances: a hole in coping, which causes a passive response in an otherwise active coper. To determine the circumstances under which a person's coping may break down, it is imperative to assess deeper levels of personality functioning.

On the surface, individuals like Tom and Sandy appear to be very confident and optimistic. But deeper down, their coping is passive. The ideal is an individual who exhibits active coping across all levels of functioning, from surface to depth, consciously controlled, semiconsciously controlled, and unconsciously controlled, across circumstances and over time.

What this suggests and I believe is that desires, fears, and conflicts that are beyond conscious control can drive and shape workplace functioning—sometimes for the worse. Under stress, when our defenses weaken, these walled-off parts of the self are much more likely to appear. If an executive's active coping rests upon passive coping, then the business runs the risk of his demonstrating passive coping at a time when the business can least afford it.

The most influential aspects of coping style operate at levels an individual can neither identify nor control. Projective techniques attempt to get at those levels. There is no pretending, no role playing, and no faking good. They do not allow a rehearsed response or canned answer. Projective techniques act as a final validity check on what an executive asserts about his abilities and motives. They make it possible to determine whether the image he presents to the world is based on a healthy, vibrant, active coping stance or whether it is defensive, reactive, or compensatory and liable to crumble when stressed.

5

Integrity

Whenever you do a thing, act as if all the world were watching.

—THOMAS JEFFERSON

What is hateful to thyself do not do to another.

—RABBI HILLEL, BABYLONIAN TALMUD,
TRACTATE *SHABBAT* 31A

INTEGRITY HAS SEVERAL DEFINITIONS, two of which are crucial to effective leadership. The first, most common definition refers to moral character and honesty. Children learn to value and respect the views and rights of others. The second, also central to my multi-level construct of active coping, refers to the state of being whole or undiminished.[1]

The two definitions are related. As I will show with examples from my work and research, integrity in both senses stems from a structure of values. A person cannot consistently act on those values if that structure of values contains holes. A hole that permits lying links the dictionary definition of integrity and active coping. If an executive lacks integrity in the sense of wholeness, the business runs the risk that the executive's coping holes or systemic passive coping on lower levels of personality structure may emerge precisely when the business is in crisis and cripple the executive's ability to lead the business through the crisis effectively.

Integrity as a moral quality is important. There are two aspects. Not having integrity is a problem because any company with liars and cheaters in its midst runs great risk. If it does not get rid of them the whole business could be brought down. In addition, having integrity becomes a positive element in a leader's effectiveness. Companies with leaders who lack integrity will be hurt.[2] An executive with integrity is more likely to have lasting effectiveness.

Let me make it clear that when talking about integrity in a moral sense, I am not arguing that honesty or fidelity predicts leadership effectiveness. An executive who beats his wife or cheats on his wife or taxes may be a highly effective leader. But in the long run, it would be reasonable to surmise that such an executive runs the risk of being perceived as less effective. Other, high-integrity executives may not want to do business with executives who seem to lack integrity.

In chapter 4, I described three levels of psychological functioning (conscious, semiconscious, and unconscious) and suggested what can happen when a person is strong on one or two of the levels but weak on the third. Such an individual lacks a stable personality structure. In order to have the first kind of integrity—principles, a moral structure on which to base one's behaviors and actions—an individual must have strength and cohesion across all three levels of psychological functioning so that the moral structure has a strong, flexible foundation on which to rest and so it will not crumble when pressured. In this sense too, the two definitions of integrity are related.

Integrity in the sense of being whole is the term I use for describing a situation where the elements of active coping work together as a whole rather than against one another. A leader can be strong in the other three elements of active coping (psychological autonomy, integrative capacity, and catalytic coping), but unless the system is structured so that they cohere, that is, unless there is integrity in the sense of wholeness, then those elements will not cohere into reliable behavior. Low integrity is accompanied by a particular set of negatives. Executives can lack psychological autonomy and get along in life, but a deficiency in integrity in the moral sense may get them fired, imprisoned, or ostracized, preventing them from using other strengths they possess. Without integrity executives risk losing the trust of those who might have given them protection, guidance, or support, and they may be on their own. Of course, people without integrity fool people all the time.

In the rest of this chapter, I will focus on integrity as a moral quality and then on the relationship between integrity in that sense and integrity as implying wholeness of mind. The parts of this chapter showing the empirical differences between higher- and lower-integrity executives will make the link between the two clear.

Leaders have a particular need for a strong grounding in integrity because they must make decisions that will affect many people, and they must make choices quickly, often without the luxury of consulting with their friends, colleagues, accountants, or attorneys. This does not mean that if they could postpone decisions and make them slowly they would not need integrity.

The integrity and self-esteem I describe in this chapter are different from the "self-esteem" of the narcissist, who cares only for himself and his self-interests and has little or no regard for the rights and perspectives of others.[3] Not all forms of self-esteem are positive; a person may score high on tests of self-esteem but be a criminal. Self-esteem in and of itself does not confer integrity, but a person cannot maintain a strong moral structure, whatever the content of the moral code, without an equally strong belief in himself and his ability to make correct choices. Individuals may be highly narcissistic and demonstrate high self-confidence but their self-confidence is a defense against an underlying sense of insecurity.

Integrity as perceived by others means that the person consistently does what he promises and has consistently acted in the appropriate way, defined in terms of the norms of the community. All of us have at least a vague idea of what is right and what is wrong, what is appropriate and what is not. Behaving with integrity may come at a cost, but it also brings rewards, or the alternative to behaving with integrity may be worse.

Here is one example of how integrity contributes to the effectiveness of a leader. The following quotation is by a former CFO of a large automotive supplier. In 2000, the bottom fell out of the market. The company went from nearly a decade of record earnings to record losses. In this context, his finance and accounting team discovered that the company had collected over $1 million more than it should have from a customer. They had not overbilled; the customer had simply paid too much.

"Nothing had been done intentionally. Somebody screwed up on the payments, and we ended up getting paid more than we should have. One day someone was reconciling our account and discovered we had this credit balance in a group of receivables from [that customer]. He asked me, 'They've never asked for it; should I just take it into income?' That was where it dawned on me that making that decision was not as simple as it seemed because everybody was watching what my response was going to be, and the ramifications were bigger than whether we kept their money or paid them back. It was going to be a basis for justifying other behaviors by other people in the company based on what I decided to do. I said, 'We've got to pay it back.' I was viewed as if I had fallen off the deep end."

This CFO sent the message to his finance team and his customer that the company would behave, at least in its financial functions, with transparency and honesty. It cost the company a million dollars, but in the long run the company strengthened its relationship with the customer—and the revenues derived from that customer.

Defining Integrity in Business

This section discusses different definitions of moral integrity. My current operational definition of integrity focuses on transparency and commitment.

By transparency, I mean that leaders who behave with integrity maintain a consistency of standards and hold themselves to a public standard. Can I feel confident that every one of my actions could be subjected to rigorous scrutiny by the press and public and be seen as creditable? This is the test of transparency.

Not only are persons of integrity less afraid of public censure; they also demonstrate commitment to a vision that is broader than self-interest. To be a person of high integrity means that you are not merely being honest, not merely willing to be transparent, but are also willing to adhere to a socially accepted set of values and ideals. *The set of values and ideals varies by society.* This is the test of commitment. As a consequence, such persons take into account the effects of their actions on others.

Integrity according to this definition is not only ethically desirable but is also a practical virtue. It is particularly important in predicting how an executive will perform. High integrity in executives reduces agency costs because you can believe what they say.[4] You can rely on them to fulfill commitments and meet accepted standards. Executives who exhibit integrity can help protect a company from illegal or unethical practices if they declare those practices illegal or unethical within their companies. Executives who live up to their internalized values and ideals may have higher self-esteem and protect shareholder value. They also uphold the good reputations of their companies. These are significant effects of this element of active coping that contribute to effective leadership.

I arrived at my current operational definition of integrity in 2008 after a great deal of study. One dictionary definition of integrity is "a firm adherence to a code of especially moral or artistic values." We should also take into account how individuals involved in business define integrity. I interviewed executives (operating executives, private equity investors, and investment bankers), a business reporter, and an attorney specializing in private equity transactions to learn how each of them would define integrity in business.

As will become apparent, each of their definitions suffers from the same fundamental weakness; it attempts to restrict integrity to a particular realm—the individual, the interpersonal, or the communal. The problem is not that the definition given is wrong but that it is partial. I believe integrity is a combination of all three. The ideal executive manifests integrity in all three realms: within himself, in relations with others, and in the life of the community. Many of the definitions refer to integrity in the sense of moral values, but we move beyond that to include the definition of integrity as a state of being whole, integral.

At one extreme, those I interviewed defined it as behaving in a manner that the person believes is right. These extremely narrow definitions of integrity locate it solely within the individual. These definitions state that integrity exists when a person's actions all derive from the same set of values.[5] Although the values may change, the congruence of these values with each other and with a person's actions determines that person's degree of integrity. One person said: "Integrity means living by your own standards, and it doesn't matter what those standards are. As long as you are consistent within that value system, you have integrity. . . . It's not a question of whether it's lawful or whether it hurts others but whether it is within your own system of values."

This definition is too narrow. Few people would consider someone who lies and cheats repeatedly to have integrity just because he believes he is doing nothing wrong. To be considered as having integrity he would have to be lying and cheating for a higher end, in service of another set of values (like an undercover agent doing his job, or like Poles who risked their lives to hide and protect Jews during World War II).

Other professionals I interviewed gave widely different interpretations, each of which was valid but insufficient. For example, one person said: "If you can genuinely say you would be happy and not ashamed to see what you are doing on the front page of the *Wall Street Journal*, in detail, right now, then you are probably behaving with integrity."

This definition touches on an important aspect of integrity but is also a partial definition. It focuses on the individual. It does not capture the whole thing. Many systems of thought prohibit killing, lying, and cheating and also take into account the context of duty. Everything we do occurs in a context of our fellow humans. Integrity *must* be broader than a private code of conduct. The extreme, narrow definition of integrity as pertaining solely to the individual suggests that we can think of it primarily as holding steadfast to our values and commitments. This definition, as stated above, is grossly inadequate. The English novelist Iris Murdoch wrote, "Love is the perception of individuals. Love is the extremely difficult realisation that something other than oneself is real."[6] Integrity involves recognizing that others share this world and that their lives are valid and not a reflection of yours. To behave with integrity is not to be manipulated by the whims of personal interest. Defining integrity as acting in ways that are consistent with one's values is fine if one's values encompass more than oneself. But defining integrity solely in ways that are consistent with one's values fails to capture the full meaning of integrity unless those values take into account the effect of the behavior on others and the duty one owes to them.

Another way of defining integrity would be to see how it operates in interpersonal relationships. One person gave this view; note that the definition takes into account the individual's obligations to others: "Integrity is not behaving in a totally self-serving way. It almost comes down to how others perceive it. Did that person act in the interest of the majority of the stakeholders, or did he act in his personal interest?"

Another person made the point that acting with integrity is acting according to the actor's own sincerely, authentically held values, subject to the requirements that the actor believes sincerely (1) that it would be good if everyone acted in accordance with the same values and (2) that these values and the actions flowing from them are moral. There can be some degree of variation in the strictness of adhering to this set of requirements in different situations. He gave the following definition: "Integrity means living by your standards, standards which you believe in and which you believe would be good if everyone followed them. It's not a question of whether it's lawful—some decisions involve moral considerations that the law does not cover. You can do very nasty things while still acting with integrity. I think the Protestants who slaughtered Catholics or the Catholics who slaughtered Protestants during the religious wars after the Reformation were not acting without integrity. They thought the whole of civilization required the elimination of those people.

"The first point is that acting with integrity is acting according to your own values. The second point is that the person who is acting with integrity believes he is acting on moral grounds. We may view them as despicable values. The third point is slightly different. At some point we all have conflicts of interests that may also be conflicts of values. High-integrity individuals are often caught in moral dilemmas. If I had been in Poland during the Holocaust, I might have decided to save Jews. But if I had children [who] were likely to be killed if I had been caught, would I be willing to risk [their] lives, and would it be morally justifiable to do that?"

Note that this definition, while focusing on the person's own standards, does not limit itself to the individual. It recognizes that every person has interpersonal relations that may constrain that person's decisions.

Integrity includes taking into account a complex web of relationships and competing interests in a suitably effective way. It reflects and respects the interests of many conflicting constituencies.

Any enterprise that has more than one person has a communal dimension. Executive decisions involve the enterprise as a whole. A definition of integrity rooted in community takes this context into account. Communities influence individual behavior by establishing norms of appropriate behavior and rules intended to prevent bad behavior.

The culture of an organization can encourage greater transparency (and other benefits) and commitment to the good of the firm, as noted by another person: "Making it okay to lay the facts and issues and truths out is organizationally what fosters integrity. We want to know all the issues right away. If you have a bad month or lose a customer, we want everyone to feel comfortable putting that on the table right away—and solving it. Then the team makes a decision, the whole firm.

"When you make a bad decision, you bring it to the board right away. Then the firm has a problem, not you. You have the information, and we have the information, and we deal with it together. That's the only thing that fosters good behavior and helps people maintain integrity. Our being one team lends itself to the right atmosphere and the right behavior.

"Sharing information doesn't mean we aren't being tough minded. If management isn't cutting it, we will deal with it ethically and with caring. But it's not like we're milquetoast, rah-rah, everyone is a fair-haired, A-player. You have to have accountability, responsibility, and you don't ignore problems."

On the other hand, there is no reason to suppose that what works for one group or organization works for another. *Each community defines morality and hence its importance in terms of its own particular social needs.*

In business, as in our everyday lives, there are different levels of community, wider levels of the social good. There is an immediate level, the local culture of the organization. There is also the social and economic environment of the organization, including larger bodies that issue regulations (for example, generally accepted accounting standards) by which all members must abide, and the law, which may be even broader. There are also ethical codes of conduct that may overlap with all of the above in various ways.

When I describe executives as having high integrity, I mean that these executives go the extra mile: they are not *just* abiding by the law, or *just* abiding by personal code of conduct, or *just* abiding by local norms. They are trying to do the right thing on every level.

We come closer to understanding how an executive demonstrates integrity in business when we link the three levels at which integrity is defined above—the individual, interpersonal, and communal definitions. No one acts in a vacuum. Every person acts in relation to other discrete individuals within a collective whole. When we act, we act within one or more communities.

Yet many executives are insulated from the effects of their decisions. They may not know how their actions affect those around them and certainly do not know how the effects of their decisions will affect those not around them. Transparency may help them see how their lives are connected to those other lives. One person put it the following way: "Integrity means learning to think with others and with others in mind. Can you talk about your actions openly? What are you trying to hide? You still need the support of a community willing to say, 'Even with the best intentions we can make mistakes.' We are not asking for people to be perfect; we are asking for people to be honest and open and reaching out to others so if things don't work out there is room for open disclosure so we can learn from it and don't do it again."

Integrity not only needs to be personal—"these are my personal standards"—or interpersonal—"how do my actions affect others"—but also communal. That recognition also brings us back to the question of what is moral. The answer to the question of which value trumps the other may depend on the context. *The context for the purposes of this book is behavior within a commercial enterprise in the United States.*

One person recounted the following story. His view is that there are explicit, unambiguous standards as to how one should act in practically every situation, but there is a degree of flexibility in how one might properly and appropriately act and still be suitably within the overall frame of the definition of proper integrity. There can be situation-specific factors that might allow behavior that might be superficially or mechanically not in accord with high integrity but are in substantive fact, genuinely in accordance with authentic integrity when the situation is viewed as a whole. This approach to integrity is analogous to the Potter Stewart approach to obscenity: "I can't define it in words, but I know it when I see it." This person's story follows below:

I was asked by a friend to teach a class on Enron in her corporate law seminar at a law school (when Enron was the big news of the day). Everybody knew how "terribly" Enron management had acted. To get the class thinking I had to shock them out of their goody-goody self-satisfaction.

So I began the class by telling them that to understand Enron they had to realize that they, like most Americans, had been taught to break the law from childhood, by their parents. They stared at me. "Well," I said, "when you were children, and your parents were driving you somewhere, did they never go over the speed limit?" (I could read "What a jerk" in their faces and body language. Everybody knows that speeding is not really breaking the law.) Pause.

I continued. "But when a police car showed up, they slowed down immediately, didn't they?" A light began to shine. "So you were eventually aware that driving over the speed limit is breaking the law, right?" "However," I continued, "they didn't drive more than maybe ten miles over the limit, not eighty or ninety miles, right?" They all agreed. (I didn't say "when you were in the car," which would have made my rhetorical question more accurate.) "Well," I explained, "the issues I want us to go into today are not how Enron came to be driving 65 in a 55-mile zone but how and why they went from 65 to 90."

But the students were not quite ready for a class on Enron, I thought, so I continued with the true story or how one night, at two in the morning, I was walking with my college-age son on the main street of Berlin. We came to a red light. There wasn't a car to be seen in any direction, so we crossed. There were two young women waiting at the light, and as we crossed we heard a sound behind us. We turned around, and there they were, running across the street against the red light, hand in hand, giggling away. As good Germans, they probably had never before crossed a street against a red light. And then I said to the class: "I would not like to live in a culture where nobody crosses the street against a red light even at two in the morning when there is no car visible in any direction." And then the class began.

Who gains if pedestrians wait for the light to change at two in the morning when no car is visible in any direction? Nobody. Who is harmed? Nobody.

As noted previously, it took a lot of time studying the field before I reached the operational definition of integrity first mentioned in this chapter. One component is transparency. Demonstrating transparency says, "I do not fear public exposure; my actions are open for others to see. Whatever the consequences may be, I do not fear them sufficiently to hide the truth." Implied in the notion of transparency are larger communal values. Transparency factors in those wider levels of goodness. To that is added the idea of a commitment to a broader vision of social or political relations. The community's perception that a person has integrity is largely based on how consistently that person behaves according to the norms of that community, particularly whether that person keeps his commitments that matter to his community. Depending on the community these may be commitments to a faith, to a professional code of conduct, or to the rigid rules that govern many criminal gangs.

Having discussed the conceptual and operational definitions of integrity in business, we now move to the second part of this chapter: the characteristics of high and low integrity in executives. The question is how organizations can select high-integrity executives and screen out charismatic yet untrustworthy executives.

To answer this question, in 2008 I designed a study, consulting with Jordan Jacobowitz, to identify and understand the differences between high- and low-integrity executives. It explored key propositions about integrity used in the first moral sense.

1. Behaving with integrity in business has two components: transparency, which means that executives maintain a consistency of standards and hold themselves to a public standard; and commitment to values that transcend personal needs and desires.

2. Integrity and psychological autonomy are two elements of the active coping personality style, and they reinforce each other. Psychological autonomy does not necessarily imply that a person has integrity, and integrity does not necessarily imply that a person has psychological autonomy, but they will be linked in those who have sufficient integrity and sufficient psychological autonomy and become stronger by virtue of being linked on both dimensions. Psychological autonomy, the ability to consider one's internal motives and values together with external information about the motives and values of others and thus to resist following just the selfish motives of the self or the pressuring demands of others, makes it more likely that a person will act with integrity. Conversely, integrity is often a major guiding factor in the decisions that a person makes autonomously.

3. Integrity in the moral sense is also structurally associated with integrative capacity and catalytic coping (two other elements of the active coping style). Integrative capacity is the ability to

perceive and incorporate the values of integrity with other perceptions and forces of the internal and external worlds. Catalytic coping relies on integrity in the moral sense (values, for example) to assure that coping behaviors and decisions are contained within an ethical framework.

4. Executives who demonstrate high integrity often have developmental histories of a loving attachment to and identification with a parent or significant other who expressed a cohesive set of values during the executives' formative years.[7] Both integrity and psychological autonomy depend on the presence of a loved and empathic authority figure during their childhood, adolescent, and young adult years. Other coping elements are linked to this as well. Loving parents or guardians who provide their children with ethical boundaries and encourage them to express themselves within those boundaries encourage the child to be aware of inner and outer experiences. This openness to awareness is the basis of integrative capacity. These parents are more likely to provide security to enable the child to seek active resolutions to conflicts and problems.[8] This security is the basis of catalytic coping.

5. Individuals who are active copers on overt and covert levels of psychological functioning find a balance between their needs and the requirements of the environment. They have the maturity to recognize that others have needs and wishes as pressing as their own.

Drawing on assessments of over two hundred candidates that I had made from 2004 to 2008, plus approximately one hundred earlier ones and whose complete test records I had recorded and saved,[9] I used my operational definition of integrity to choose six executives whose behavior over the course of their lives as evidenced in the histories they reported to me during the assessment and in their subsequent actions showed high integrity. Also using the two tests of integrity, I chose six executives who demonstrated low integrity. For example, four of the six reported that they committed fraud in their past roles as executives; two of the four were asked to resign. A third member of this group of four boasted throughout the interview of a life history of repetitive, astonishing fraud and embezzlement—and of never being caught.

I then compared the psychological characteristics of the six executives who showed high integrity to those who exhibited low integrity. I was looking for what differentiated the members of the two groups that would allow me to predict, based on data that I could obtain in advance, whether other executives would demonstrate integrity throughout their careers. And what I found was enough to help me predict the probability of integrity when conducting subsequent assessments.

Let me repeat that I defined integrity in terms of two components: Transparency, accepting the risk of public exposure; and commitment, the ability to stick to a vision or values that extend beyond the self, that take into account the good of the community, not just the good of the self. I used the same two components of integrity to identify executives who reliably fit the high-integrity group. The first was whether the person maintained a consistency of standards rather than behaving according to a wavering set of standards. This was the test of transparency. This test rules out lying, deception, and using insider knowledge to manipulate others for personal gain. The second was whether the person demonstrated commitment to a vision or set of values that extended beyond the self. This was the test of commitment.

I used the same two components to identify low-integrity executives—those who had behaved in a self-serving way, using hidden, deceitful sets of standards (for example, keeping at least two sets of books), and who had sought to manipulate and deceive investors, stockholders, lenders, customers, and employees. In other words, they flunked the tests of transparency and commitment. Over the course of determining whether an executive showed higher or lower integrity, there were areas of tension when values conflicted: greyness, not black and white, not right and wrong.

As stated above, I chose six executives who fit the definition of high integrity and six who did not. My review occurred at least five years after the original assessment of the candidate. The data I considered included the executive's developmental histories, measures of cognitive ability, and behaviors on the various other data collection instruments used in the assessment as well as behaviors demonstrated by the executive subsequent to the original assessment. I interviewed industry colleagues, superiors, and peers of each executive to provide third-party data that would confirm or refute my classification of that executive as having higher or lower integrity. I then reviewed the executives' developmental and personality data in an effort to identify what differentiated executives who would behave with consistently high integrity from those who would not.

After analyzing the assessment data in collaboration with Jordan Jacobowitz, some very specific patterns emerged. Not only were there striking differences between the two groups; we also noted a high degree of internal consistency within each group. The two groups were superficially very similar in that they had been presented to me as candidates for hiring or promotion to more senior leadership roles.

I will call the higher-integrity executives Bill, George, Isaac, Ken, Nick, and Scott and the lower-integrity executives Brad, Geoff, Sandy, Ned, Mitch, and Jerry. These are not their real names. How did these executives perform on the various instruments used to collect data about their functioning?

Findings

Intelligence, Education, and Experience

The high-integrity executives tended to score higher on a measure that taps abstract reasoning.[10] This test identifies differences among individuals who score more than two standard deviations of the mean on the normal IQ test, yielding differences in level of ability within an already bright population. It has a range from 0 to 36. Four of the six high-integrity executives scored 26 or higher, whereas only one of six of the low-integrity group did. Rounding up for both groups, the high-integrity executives achieved a mean of 28; the mean for the low-integrity executives was 22.[11] (The mean for CEOs who were nominated for participation in the study on successful CEOs of private equity–funded ventures was 24 with a standard deviation of 5.)

This finding *suggests* a link between integrity and abstract thinking.[12] If one has a high degree of abstract thinking to draw upon to deal with complex situations, one is more likely to find solutions to ethical dilemmas that do not harm others or break the law.

I made no *formal, in-depth* evaluation of the quality of the executives' functional skills. That is not my purview. All executives who come to me for assessment have met basic criteria related to industry experience and functional skills of executive recruiters, investors, boards of directors, or executives making the hiring decision. All twelve described themselves as having done well enough in school to move on, with education having an instrumental purpose. All had at least an undergraduate degree; seven possessed an advanced degree. Their academic and professional performance was sufficient to advance to the general management level or above. As stated previously, on the surface, the two groups appeared very similar in terms of intelligence and education.

The personality characteristics found when analyzing the two groups began to appear more clearly in their work histories. The higher-integrity executives tended to be steadily upwardly mobile, loyal to their employers, and well regarded within their industries. The lower-integrity executives tended to quit, be fired, or join unstable organizations, and they had frequent disagreements with their bosses. These latter tendencies may have been partly a function of intelligence—that is, failure to fathom sufficiently the social nature of the organizations they joined—and partly a function of their failure to utilize their coping potential.[13]

Developmental Histories of the High- and Low-Integrity executives

I take two perspectives when I look at a person's development. The first relates to the individual's past, how his or her personality developed during childhood and through adolescence and early adulthood. This perspective helps explain the person's motivations. The second looks at the subject's current developmental conditions (for example, marriage, children, sustaining social relationships). This perspective is also useful in explaining and predicting the person's behavior.

In general, the higher-integrity executives described having loving, warm relationships with adults in their childhoods. Children's identifications with idealized adults play a major role in the formation of integrity, particularly the way in which a developing self is partly based upon identifications with these role models. The high-integrity executives also tended to describe their current family lives as harmonious and happy.

The lower-integrity executives, on the other hand, emphasized childhood tensions between themselves and the adults in their lives. These deficits left a vacuum of attachments for the low-integrity executives in their youth, and these executives instead developed a hyperindependent stance toward the world, cutting themselves off from potential sources of support, whether by authority figures (teachers, coaches, friendly neighbors) or peers. These low-integrity executives also used less positive terms in describing their current family and marital situations.

Personality Structure and Dynamics

Having summarized the differences between the higher- and lower-integrity executives in terms of their developmental history, let us look at them in terms of personality structure—their drives and the defenses against them. I will begin with the self-report level of motivational priorities. The executives completed a self-report test designed to identify their motivational priorities and patterns.[14] On this measure of personality, they all fell within the normal range of the population. In that sense, on the surface they were very similar.

Nevertheless, other personality characteristics on the self-report measure of personality differentiated the higher- and lower-integrity groups. Compared to the lower-integrity executives, the responses of the higher-integrity executives indicated that they were more respectful of the needs of others and more self-controlled and humble. Conversely, the responses of the lower-integrity executives indicated that they were more motivated to rebel against authority and conventional expectations, to act in accordance with their immediate impulses and desires without full consideration of the possible consequences, and to promote themselves in social situations, seeking admiration. Overall, the lower-integrity executives showed less inclination to balance their personal needs with the needs of others.

Next, let us look at the coping tendencies exhibited by the two groups. I used the sentence completion technique described in chapter 4 and appendix B to measure coping tendencies at the semiprojective level of behavior. Recall that semiprojective measures yield more spontaneous and less consciously controlled depictions of personality, at least in comparison to structured, objective, self-report tests such as personality inventories.

The motivational differences on the self-report measure of personality relate to and reflect the differences in their developmental histories—for instance, the early relationships between the executives and their fathers. The lower-integrity executives had conflicts with their fathers. This factor contributed to their exhibitionistic, rebellious, and impulsive motivational structures. They appeared to reject the presence and legitimacy of authority. They trusted only themselves, believing that whatever impulsive action they took would be successful and praiseworthy. The profiles of the higher-integrity executives indicated that compared to the lower-integrity group they were more empathic and respectful of others. Their respect for their fathers carried over to the value they placed on authority figures as well as to their being able to function as inspiring authority figures for others. Motivation appeared to go hand in hand with the coping styles developed by the two groups.

I found a distinct difference between the higher-integrity executives and the others on the semiprojective measure of coping. Sixty-seven percent of the higher-integrity executives had the highest final score (five) possible on this test, compared to only 33 percent of the lower-integrity executives. No high-integrity executive received a final score lower than four (which corresponds to at least average adaptive coping); 50 percent of the low-integrity executives did.

Although the higher-integrity executives tended to have higher scores overall on the semiprojective measure of coping, the findings were mixed. Some of the lower-integrity executives also had very high scores on this measure, but the content and motivations on display were quite divergent between the two groups. The trends noted on the self-report test recurred on the semiprojective measure. The higher-integrity executives exhibited a fairly consistent balance between meeting their own needs and the needs of others. They also stressed their commitment to maintaining ethical behavior and their disdain for those who do not.

By contrast, lower-integrity executives emphasized a powerful desire to function independently, often expressing a fear of becoming passively dependent on others. They tended to view themselves in a highly positive manner that bordered on the grandiose, as faultless and perfect. Their grandiosity was related to the exhibitionism (the desire to be the center of attention) that they expressed on the self-report measure of personality. They mistrusted others and lacked respect for them.

Combining the motives expressed on the self-report measures and the semiprojective measures, it is noteworthy that all twelve executives valued independence, *but the members of the lower-integrity group saw it as their defining character trait*. They valued their independence over their personal relationships (a characteristic associated with narcissism but not definitive of low integrity) and would rather tell other people what to do than collaborate with them.

What did the assessment data show about motivation and coping at the deeper levels of personality? The source of these widely diverging motivations becomes apparent when looking at the themes expressed by the executives on the projective storytelling test.

In order to access the deepest level of psychological functioning—the bottom of the iceberg, as it were—I assess every executive I evaluate using the same projective storytelling technique. As described in chapter 4 and appendix B, this technique assesses motives, interpersonal styles, conflicts, coping tendencies, and personality characteristics such as self-esteem, confidence, and conscientiousness that may or may not have been evident at the self-report level. The stories help build an individualized profile for each executive. These profiles aided my understanding of how each executive integrated—on conscious and unconscious levels—his internal needs, his past history, and his current work, family, and social spheres.

The projective stories consistently differentiated the two groups. Executives within the higher-integrity group created very rich and active stories in response to this technique. Their stories indicated that they were psychologically organized in a secure, resilient, and self-satisfied way. The executives with lower integrity created poor stories. Their stories revealed underlying areas of defensiveness and vulnerability, making them more limited in their abilities to function in a consistent and effective manner.

Let us look at the ways a particular story or expression by an executive is evidence of identification with a parental figure and the ways in which that provides a foundation of psychological cohesiveness that becomes the basis for active coping.

I will begin with stories in response to the picture of a young boy contemplating a violin that rests on a table in front of him. The first high-integrity CEO—Scott, who also appeared in chapter 1—told the following story to describe what he saw:

> Billy was infatuated with the violin ever since his grandfather took him to the philharmonic. He often stared at the violin that his grandfather purchased from the Salvation Army in hopes that he would learn to play well. He was frustrated by the fact that he knew that his family could not afford to pay for lessons and this would be something that he would have to learn later on in life. In junior high school, he had the opportunity to take lessons and became proficient very quickly. The original violin his grandfather bought for him five years ago lay in his room as inspiration to fulfill his dream. Billy attended Julliard on a full scholarship because of his ability and mastery of the instrument and became the concertmaster for the New York Philharmonic and as a side note, when he fixed up that old violin that his grandfather gave him, it turned out to be a forgotten Stradivarius that rewarded him for his diligence.

One noticeable characteristic of this story is the identification of the central character, Billy, with a male parental figure, the grandfather. This identification consistently motivates the character's aspirations and achievement. The character displays an active coping stance by identifying his desire to play the violin, working hard, and fulfilling his dream despite obstacles. In the end, he also attains a sense of great satisfaction as a reward for his diligent practice. Ultimately, the self (Billy's desires), the other (grandfather's wishes), and the community (the New York Philharmonic) come together in a harmonious fashion. Noteworthy too is the story's organization, complexity, sequential logic, and cultural sophistication.

Here's the response to the same picture by another CEO, Brad:

> This is a kid who is supposed to be practicing his violin, sheet music is in front of him; his buddies are outside. He's been forced to do it, told to go to his room and get it done, and he's struggling with the concept he doesn't want to do it because he's been told to but if he doesn't do it he's not going to do these other things and he's trying to come to terms with that but he hasn't made the decision yet to pick the damn thing up and play it.

This is a low-integrity story. Not only is there no parental identification figure, but there is also an implied hostile or resentful relationship with the undefined authority figure ("He's been forced to do it"). The character's motivation is at odds with the "other," and there is no resolution to that implied conflict ("he hasn't made the decision yet"). He does not negotiate with his parents and come up with a compromise that would fulfill their demands and also satisfy what he wants to do. The main character is stuck between complying with an external demand and following his desires (but does not actually state what those desires are). He even displaces or transfers his resentment from the parental figures to the violin (work): "the damn thing." He is conflicted. Brad's story is structurally less complex than Scott's story, and the language and rhetoric are also simpler.

Another picture is a farm scene: in the foreground is a young woman with books in her hand; in the background is a man working the fields while an older woman looks on. Scott narrated the following story:

> Heather was always a bright girl and was often called a prodigy in school. Upon the completion of high school she received a full scholarship to Harvard University and elected to continue onto the Harvard Business School where she envisioned herself entering Corporate America. She graduated summa cum laude, was well received with many encouraging offers of opportunity, but upon her father's request and because of her devotion to him, returned to their Mormon farm to lead the family after her mother had passed away. She often wonders what life could have been.

Tension between self and other is a theme in this story. Despite great success, the central character sacrifices her burgeoning career to meet the needs and expectations of her family. There is a faint recognition at the end that this culturally laudatory act is not ideal, as it does not bring about a satisfying balance between her dreams and her duty. Nevertheless, responsibility takes precedence over self-development. Like the first story told by Scott, this one is well organized and logical. To the same picture, Brad gave the following response:

> This looks like a rural family. Appears to be more of the old classic cultural norms where the man is working in the field but this one, the woman appears to be teaching or going off to school; looks like the old schoolmarm type. A lot of stereotypical types of appearances here: the guy without a shirt on working in the field, the lady who's pregnant, the woman like I said with the books, so it might be like I said, the school teacher has come to visit. [Examiner query: What are characters doing, thinking, and feeling?] He's plowing the field. No one looks overjoyed about the situation. The man has his back to the lady so he's obviously not taking interest in her; the lady with her

back against the tree is looking off into the distance and not really involved with either what was said or what is about to be said unless she is truly in deep thought, she just seems detached from what is going on; and the woman with the books, there's a stoic look on her face so what has transpired or what is about to transpire she doesn't seem to be too emotional about the fact so either way it doesn't seem to be a major issue here.

In this somewhat disjointed story, the characters are unrelated to one another, each in their own world. They are defined in a "stereotypical" manner. They are disconnected ("not taking interest"; "detached"), unfeeling, and dissatisfied ("no one looks overjoyed about the situation"). To a picture that most executives see as a family scene, this CEO indirectly expressed a deep-seated feeling of familial coldness and disinterest. Stylistically, Brad struggled to construct a story to this picture, and I had to prompt him to elaborate and complete his story.

What were the performance outcomes associated with Scott and Brad? Scott leads the second-biggest company in his investor's current portfolio. He persevered to ensure that the company and its investors were well served. He has completely repositioned the company in the industry, and he is now focusing on grooming successor candidates to be ready to take control when he leaves, which he expects to be in the foreseeable future.

The company prospered and grew under Brad's leadership, but in the end his lack of integrity and the qualities noted in his projective stories (characters are detached and do not communicate with one another, he does not perceive what most respondents perceive as a family unit, and he reveals hostility toward authority figures) caused the company significant harm. He left the company after less than two years as its CEO after being offered a more lucrative position. Without informing the original investors or the new ones of the offer and that he had accepted it, he induced his investors to inject more capital into the company by bringing in a new set of equity sponsors. One board observer reported feeling betrayed by Brad's failure to communicate to the board that he would be quitting. Another board member reported that the employees felt betrayed, as well. Because no one wanted him around once he announced his intention to leave, his departure was fast. Without Brad as CEO, the company's performance faltered. He had not developed a successor nor given investors sufficient time to find an adequate replacement.

Summary—Personality Structure and Dynamics

The major difference between the two groups appeared in their projective stories. As explained in chapter 4, projective techniques provide information about the foundation of personality structure. The overwhelming majority of the lower-integrity group, regardless of how they appeared in person, told problematic stories. In five of the six cases, the stories gave evidence of interpersonal issues, personality disorganization, and problems with self-esteem and maintaining an integral sense of self.

Analyses of the stories told by high- and low-integrity CEOs, combined with data from their self-report and semiprojective measures and developmental histories, indicate distinct differences in their psychological structures. High-integrity executives connected to the people around them, identified with benevolent and caring paternal figures, and linked those identifications with their needs for self-development. This fusion ultimately resulted in genuine concern for the communities they served. By contrast, low-integrity executives felt rejected by authorities, tended to suppress warm feelings toward others, developed defensively independent lifestyles, and felt entitled to pursue their self-interests at the expense of those around them.

More specifically, high-integrity executives consistently articulated and resolved conflicts between others and within themselves (for example, torn between duty and obligation or conflicts between complying with the expectations of parents and with what they truly desire). They found a way to balance their own desires for self-development with the expectations of their families and society. For example, they showed how they could negotiate their needs with others and submerge their feelings to defer to the greater good of the family. Themes of integrity and altruism were woven throughout their life histories, sentence completion tests, and projective stories in the references they made to charitable motives and standing up for what was right.

By contrast, the lower-integrity executives were unable to arrive at or even consider resolutions between their own needs and those of others. Some of them referred to other human beings as if they were objects to be circumvented or used for self-gratification and not as true individuals, independent centers of initiative, much less individuals worth emulating. Other low-integrity executives specifically denied conflicts between themselves and the outside environment. Similar to the trends noted on the other assessment measures, the characters in their projective stories struggled with authority figures, often denigrating them. Their characters' high needs for autonomy and rebelliousness, coupled with self-centeredness and interpersonal ambivalence, blocked pathways to finding ways to live peacefully with others.

The defensive nature of their independence appeared on all levels: This is the congruence discussed in chapter 4. We see it in their projective stories, where the characters are viewed as isolated. We see it on the surface, where they expressed a preference for being on their own; they did not like to be told what to do. Growing up, they had no choice but to rely on themselves. They experienced themselves as alone and apart from other people. This quality differs strikingly from that of the high-integrity executives, who convey a sense of basic trust and formed strong attachments throughout their lives.

Also noteworthy were systematic differences in the way high-integrity and low-integrity executives constructed their stories. High-integrity executives generally created long, complex, coherent, and well-organized stories. Lower-integrity executives mostly produced disjointed, illogical, underdeveloped, and incomplete stories. These stylistic differences indicated clear psychological differences in the degree of self-organization between the higher- and lower-integrity executives.

On the surface, the lower-integrity executives were self-adulating and consciously flaunted their needs for autonomy as strengths. Yet such tendencies in their projective stories led to unresolved conflicts with authority figures and a failure to find satisfactory ways to relate to others or to promote the self adaptively. By contrast, the high-integrity executives consistently imagined ways of integrating altruistic and achievement-oriented motives. The foundation of integrity seemed most observable in the expressed fantasies of the executives, on the covert measures of personality.

Again, as described in chapter 4, each executive's coping is scored on the three methods used to assess personality: self-report, semiprojective, and projective, which correspond to three levels of behavior: conscious, semiconscious, and unconscious. Each level is then categorized as "H" (high level of functioning), "Medium" or "M," or "L" (low level of functioning).

The high integrity executives were consistently high across all methods of assessment—the HHH type. By contrast, only one of the lower-integrity executives was the HHH type. In general, the low-integrity executives *presented* themselves in a very good light; some seemed energetic and effective on the semiprojective measure (the sentence completion test), although not all of them; and only *one* showed active coping on the projective measure. In other words, the deeper one probed into their personality structures, the more conflicted, passive, disorganized, and troubled they appeared.

These lower-integrity executives built their personas into big, impressive edifices that look strong from the outside, but for all but one, their unconscious coping—the foundation of their personalities—is as weak as shifting sand. Under stress, the façades of these five may crumble, and they grasp at any means—ethical or no—to prevent psychological collapse.

Companies have a choice prior to making an investment in an executive. One is to do what they usually do—look at the executive's past performance. The past is a good predictor of how executives will deal with circumstances they've met in the past. But executives today will find themselves in different circumstances tomorrow—perhaps from stiffer competition in a consolidating industry, a flagging economy, technological changes, new owners, a new management team, or a new customer base. Every change in circumstance creates additional stress, which can push executives who lack a firm structure of integrity to behave in ways that are destructive and unethical. The methods of assessment described in this book can add accuracy to the prediction of managerial performance by identifying whether an executive is likely to cope under stress with integrity.

6

Psychological Autonomy
Lemmings Need Not Apply

Any fool can make things bigger, more complex, and more violent.
It takes a touch of genius—and a lot of courage—to move in the
opposite direction.

—ALBERT EINSTEIN

ANOTHER CRUCIAL ELEMENT OF ACTIVE coping is psychological autonomy, a vital quality for making decisions that may be
unpopular but are right. Psychological autonomy is the shield that
enables a mature, healthy person to face life with relative objectiv-
ity. It has two sides. One is empathy: I understand and try to have
sympathy for the motives of others. The other is independence
and self-awareness: I am not a lemming, I am aware of my inner
drives, and I try to understand my motives.

To have psychological autonomy a person must be aware of
internal and external pressures that are likely to influence his
views and ability to make critical decisions. Psychological autonomy involves the ability to consider the immediate pressures of
the business and its stakeholders—the demands of shareholders,
board members, customers, suppliers, employees, and the different
divisions of the business, to mention only a few. It also involves
awareness of internal pressures. A positive internal pressure could
be the desire to achieve. A destructive internal pressure could be the
compulsion to be perfect or the insatiable need to gain validation

from other people. A positive external pressure could be compliance with the law. A negative external pressure could be a self-centered, manipulative boss demanding to have his own way or a tyrannical regime that has no morals. A person who lacks the freedom to choose how to act is more prone to capitulate to groupthink, fads, or inner compulsions (such as the compulsion to win).

Responding to each of these demands and pressures to achieve success is difficult and requires considerable self-awareness and awareness of others. It is a quality possessed by an effective diplomat, a good statesman, a good lawyer, and a good investor.

Psychological autonomy includes the willingness to go beyond the status quo or to evolve values that add complexity to those learned during one's youth (that is, one is not programmed for life during early socialization, and we continue to be free to choose new values and ideals), and it is especially important to those in positions of leadership.

The world-famous research psychologist Irving Janis described a phenomenon that can occur when members of small policy-making in-groups are working under extreme stress. In these conditions, seeking consensus often becomes an overriding norm. To maintain self-esteem and group cohesion, members of the group seek validation from one another. In most groups, this phenomenon occurs to some extent even when group members are not working under extreme stress. In citing the decision making that can lead to conformity of thought and flawed decision making, Janis used a term coined by William H. Whyte in 1952—groupthink.[1] Groupthink can lead to impaired reality testing and impaired moral judgment.

A historical example: Arthur Schlesinger, one of John F. Kennedy's senior advisors, objected strenuously to the Bay of Pigs invasion in a memorandum to Kennedy but did not voice those objections during team meetings. Schleschinger later said ruefully, "In the months after the Bay of Pigs I bitterly reproached myself for having kept so silent during those crucial discussions in the cabinet room." He continued his expression of remorse: "I can only explain my failure to do more than raise a few timid questions by reporting that one's impulse to blow the whistle on this nonsense was simply undone by the circumstances of the discussion." In line with the thesis that group pressure can undermine effective leadership, management theorists have, since the 1970s, stressed the importance of a leader's vision and the ability to create and inculcate strong values that direct the actions of members of the organization.

Researchers from a variety of theoretical perspectives have also looked at the relationship between the personality of the leader and the norms of the group. Despite widely differing assumptions, these researchers generally agree that effective leaders are distinct from other group members in their capacity to adopt and promote unconventional attitudes, values, and goals, again an example of leaders' capacity for psychological autonomy.

The research psychologist E. P. Hollander advanced the idea of "idiosyncrasy credit," which means the freedom of valued group members to deviate from group norms.[2] Leaders earn this credit by displaying competent behaviors that make them indispensable. Idiosyncrasy credits allow leaders to introduce into the group's culture innovative ideas and ways of doing things, creating adaptability and change. Similarly, studies on behaviors of managers showed that charismatic managers—that is, those most likely to be transformational leaders—displayed high sensitivity for changing the status quo and "unconventional and counter-normative behavior."[3] Such managers anticipate the reactions of those in the group to significant changes in established practices and resist the temptation to capitulate to group pressures to conform.

Research on leadership traits provides additional evidence for the importance of a leader's ability to formulate and maintain relatively independent values within the context of the group. Traits that have been empirically correlated with leadership effectiveness include defiance of the sentiments of associates, self-reliance, high self-esteem, and introversion (a tendency to process one's thoughts and feelings internally, to be more private and less socially outgoing and presumably more aware of one's inner drives and biases).[4]

From a psychoanalytic vantage point, the theorist Abraham Zaleznik differentiated leaders from mere managers in terms of a "sense of separateness from the environment" and a self-confidence deriving from an "awareness of who they are and the visions that drive them to achieve."[5] For Zaleznik, creative executives are those who move beyond the accepted body of knowledge of how to do things, establishing innovative programs, ideas, and actions.[6]

General Grant provides an outstanding example of Zaleznik's thesis. The Civil War writer Noah Andre Trudeau, interviewed in *Civil War* magazine, made this insightful observation: "The way I would characterize [Grant's] Overland Campaign [in 1864 against Robert E. Lee] is that it was perhaps the first campaign in which the individual battles mattered less than the ultimate result of the campaign. Grant worried less about winning or losing a battle than he did about whether he had been diverted from his ultimate goal." In this sense, too, Grant's leadership of the Union army illustrates the creativity that feeds both psychological autonomy *and* catalytic coping, the subject of chapter 8.

Psychological autonomy is the ability to resist external pressures or internal desires or fears automatically. Instead, you maintain an objective stance to decide with full consciousness on the best course of response. At the same time, you retain a sense of yourself as an independent agent and center of initiative.[7] In perceiving both the internal (to the self) and external environments, it resembles the other elements of active coping, defined as an attribute of personality structure. Hence repetition regarding openness to internal and external sources of information will be necessary in the chapters describing the four elements of active coping.

Psychological Autonomy in CEOs

The chief executive of a company is a person who is uniquely responsible for satisfying a great many conflicting interests: the shareholders (who may also have conflicting interests among themselves), the employees, the customers, the different divisions of the corporation viewed as independent business units, the suppliers— and do it all while believing that he is pursuing the best course of action. Constituents form an ever-widening ring of responsibility for the CEO. Most narrowly, they include only the shareholders. More broadly, they include the creditors. Still more broadly, they include the community. And most broadly they include the ecology of the environment in which the business functions.

CEOs must be able to appreciate the needs and values of each of these groups to whom they owe legal duties or, more broadly speaking, moral duties. A CEO should run the corporation as profitably as possible for the shareholders while taking into account the interests of most or all of the other constituencies. To be effective, a CEO cannot become a captive or sole representative of one constituency nor become fully independent or arbitrary and rejecting of any constituency. Instead, he must function as a leader or intermediary who employs lucid reasoning and an unfaltering sense of integrity.

Leadership is at least partly a process of social exchange in which effectiveness depends on the leader's capacity to define and maintain relatively independent values. Whereas other group members are relatively more invested in the status quo, a leader who can bring about change has the autonomy to be critical of normative beliefs ("we've always thought this way") and established practices ("we've always done it this way").

A leader cannot be too independent of the group but must find a balance between independent thought and vision and harmonious, constructive cooperation. Indeed, the vision of a leader should reflect the integration of personal aims and constructive group goals. Psychological autonomy is quite different from self-destructive independence, as we will now see with Simon.

Lack of Psychological Autonomy Versus Ideal Psychological Autonomy

Simon was originally hired to replace the founder of a software company. Investors had hoped to ramp up the company's revenues significantly and exit in three years. Simon was hired to lead this growth. Over time, however, investors became displeased with Simon's leadership. His relationships with his board and management team deteriorated. This led to high turnover in his management team, which investors attributed to subordinates' mistrust of Simon as well as to his abrasive, accusatory, and demeaning interpersonal style. Also, Simon preferred very aggressive growth plans (both organic and inorganic) that required a significant cash burn and involved taking even more risk with a business that historically had healthy margins and always ran above breakeven. These plans required additional capital, which was dilutive to existing investors.

Sometimes executives are given incentives such as promises of bonuses or stock options, which would make them wealthy by their standards if the company grew rapidly and substantially. This is in effect an incentive for CEOs not to sit on their behinds. Simon was given options that would make him a lot of money if the company increased in value very substantially. Simon's investors believed that this scenario (which was their doing) led Simon to swing for the fences when a nice single or double would have been preferable from an investor's standpoint.

Simon hired me to evaluate him; he was intent on improving his chances of success. My assessment of Simon indicated that he possessed the intellectual ability and technical knowledge to succeed as CEO. On the surface, he appeared decisive, energetic, highly motivated to achieve, and active in his problem solving. But the psychological assessment revealed a major weakness in his leadership. Simon lacked psychological autonomy. He would ignore the expectations of others in his single-minded pursuit of goals that were ultimately self-aggrandizing. The flaws I found may seem to be aspects of his personality that would be noticed by anyone interviewing him in the usual fashion—but they are not. Simon had a lifetime of experience presenting a façade of willingness to cooperate with those in a position to hire him. This is not how he acted on the job. When investors got to know him, they experienced him as very difficult to manage.

In discussions with his investors and employees, a picture began to emerge of a man who was highly critical and intolerant of subordinates. In fact, in the interview he admitted these tendencies to me. At the same time, he was disappointed and dismissive of authority figures. He felt tremendous pressure to be perfect and displaced his need for perfection onto subordinates. But their performance never reached perfection. Rather than question his own leadership style, he lashed out at his direct reports. Turnover was high, but he attributed that fact to the company's geographic location, not his leadership style.

Simon also did not trust authority figures to be able to help him. He therefore felt a need to push ahead to achieve his own agenda independently. This lack of trust in others meant he had to be vigilant to defend his own interests. His psychological autonomy was so weak that he could not withstand any contradictions long enough to forge compromises. Instead, he pushed through his agenda, viewing others as weak or misguided. He lacked psychological autonomy in the crippling sense that he could not integrate the feelings and desires of coworkers and investors with his own needs. He thereby sowed the seeds of mistrust throughout his organization and with his board. To understand these observations more thoroughly, now let us look at some of the facts of Simon's own history and psychology.

Simon's inability to blend his own self-interest and concern with interest in and concern for others probably derived from his ambivalent relationship with his father. As a child, Simon, fourth among five siblings, experienced his father as a distant, demanding, critical, and demeaning disciplinarian. Simon told me he tried to satisfy his father by striving for perfection. These attempts never met with his father's approval. Simon's efforts to rebel by engaging in arguments with and confronting his father were equally ineffective in gaining his father's attention. Simon told me that he felt that his father was jealous of and denigrated Simon's achievements.

Understandably, Simon reacted by developing an ingrained feeling that he must function independently of his father and, later, of all authority figures. Unconsciously, though, he still sought his father's approval and love. He identified with his father, taking on many of his traits. For example, he adopted his father's critical and authoritarian style by becoming a demanding, dissatisfied disciplinarian at work. His subordinates could never satisfy his expectations in much the same way Simon could never satisfy his father. Tense relations with his subordinates led to the high turnover rate that concerned his investors. Simon's refusal to listen to his investors reflected his mistrust of all authority figures and his need to function and push ahead in accord with his own desires. His behavior led to a situation where he feared that investors were tempted to fire him, much the same way he felt dismissed and rejected by his father. His fears turned into a self-fulfilling prophecy; his investors did fire him. In Simon's case, the assessment helped him gain more self-awareness but not enough to overcome the effects of his formative years.

In contrast, George, one of the high-integrity executives discussed in chapter 4, exhibited psychological autonomy throughout his illustrious career. He was one of the first Americans on the senior management team of a premier Japanese firm. Once there, he demonstrated his ability to blend personal ambition with sensitivity to other business cultures. Later, as CEO, he led several venture-backed technology firms to great success.

He demonstrated both integrity and psychological autonomy when he resigned from a company that he had led successfully to the point where it was ready to go public. As CEO of that company, he and his operating team had worked diligently to line up top investment banks to take the company public. Then, at the eleventh hour, the board chairman decided to use an alternative investment bank, one with which he had a personal connection with its key banker. George refused on the grounds that he and his team had established and committed to a bank selection process. They had told the candidate banks that the selection would be made using that process. When the chairman insisted on using a bank outside the group that George and his team had identified, George resigned, walking away from millions of dollars. He was aware of his regret over the loss of so much money but was also aware of his values and reputation. He could not fight the chairman because the chairman controlled the board of directors.

The chairman's high-handedness was part of a pattern of behavior that George had long resisted. George functioned fully in an autonomous manner, aware of his motives and values, seeking compromise and harmony in most situations, until he encountered a situation that crucially violated his sense of personal integrity, at which time he decided to follow the standard he set for himself, his team, and the banking community.

George's psychological assessment indicated that he possessed the same level of intellectual ability as Simon. Like Simon, George described himself as achievement-oriented, assertive, and focused, with a desire to lead others. He wrote that he "always wanted to be looked up to and to be successful." But in contrast to Simon, George exhibited two critically important characteristics. One was a strong desire to care for others, even those who were not family. The other was a salient foundation of high ethical values.

He exuded an intense, almost palpable sense of integrity. He said, "I admire integrity, trust, loyalty" and saw his future as "helping other potential executives to succeed in a high-integrity manner."

His ability to blend competitive and achievement-oriented needs with concerns for the welfare of others while maintaining his personal integrity also was evident on the indirect measures of personality. For example, as we saw in chapter 4, in his stories to the projective storytelling test, he generated story after story about humanists who faced the challenges of meeting the expectations and needs of others while pursuing and achieving their own ambitions. Their ambitions tended to be embedded in socially useful activities, such as medicine, the arts, and business.

As with Simon, the roots of George's personality structure can be traced to his upbringing. Like Simon, George grew up in a large family, with five siblings. Unlike Simon, George described his father in unequivocally positive terms. Like the characters in George's stories, George's father was a humanist. He was a "visionary and dreamer" who "could care less about the social scene" and "could take an unpleasant situation and see the positives in it no matter how bad it was." He came from a devout Quaker family and was a conscientious objector to war. Yet, ironically, his father married a woman who came from a family of military generals. George's mother, unlike George's father, was, as characterized by George, "driven," "tough as nails," "an A++ type of personality," and "a phenomenal artist" who had been "programmed all her life to marry into wealth." Despite the temperamental and philosophical differences, or maybe because of them, his parents never fought: "They were the epitome of compromise." They "worked and played together as opposites" and were "devoted to their kids."

George internalized aspects of both of his parents, the ambition and feistiness of his mother and the integrity and humanity of his father. They served as living and powerful examples of ongoing compromise in a marriage. By observing them, he learned how to compromise, to blend what on the surface were conflicting tendencies into workable solutions. The core of psychological autonomy is the ability to recognize, to respect, and to integrate the wishes and views of others while pursuing your own goals and preserving your individuality. George is an outstanding example of psychological autonomy.

Reflections on Psychological Autonomy

Psychological autonomy, like the other elements of active coping, continues to develop throughout a person's life. One CFO, describing the experience of psychological autonomy, put it the following way, acknowledging first the internal awareness of his feelings and motives:

> That psychological discomfort that comes with seeing clearly when everyone else wants to ignore the pitfalls is not easy to tolerate. In fact, I'm never completely comfortable. I am always weighing these tensions ranging from wanting to be accepted personally, to being responsible for the risk the company is taking, to overcoming anxiety. But in a leadership position, if you don't have the ability to tolerate those tensions, by definition you can't lead. Not speaking up when you should, just keeping your head down, is not leadership. Some people adopt a belligerent attitude and just run over whoever is in front of them. Early in my career I probably opted for that approach more often than not, but as I've gained experience, I've got all the tools in my kit. I know when to press, when to be aggressive, when to back off, when to be conciliatory, when to consult, when to defer and avoid the confrontation, and when to pick it up at a more appropriate time. You have to have all those tools in your tool kit, but they originate in that soundness, that autonomy, that you're okay making decisions yourself.

The same CFO gave one illustration of his psychological autonomy at play in vetting a prospective acquisition that was twice
the size of his company and on the financial pages every day, with
four major investment banks like Solomon Smith Barney and
Credit Suisse vying for the deal.

> We were sucked in by the glamour of the transaction. A lot
> of people were blowing smoke. That's when I've always known
> to look for the ultimate simplicity.
>
> When I began to get even on the fringes of the risk assessment,
> I thought, "Wow. This thing has a tremendous number of pitfalls,
> and we're ignoring everything just because of the magnitude of the
> transaction." I didn't say anything until it became evident that we
> were actually going to do this deal without doing any diligence.
> Then I said to the CEO, "I can't do that. I'm the Chief Financial
> Officer of the company. If I don't sound the alarm bell nobody
> else will." I was comfortable that this was the right thing to do.
> It met the test of logic: how do you do a transaction when you
> don't have any information? In fact, how do you explain to the
> investors why you did this deal when you didn't look at anything?

As this example shows, the CFO cited "was comfortable that this
was the right thing to do." He was aware of his inner feelings as
well as the external parameters of his role.

The final example, below, gives this CFO's thoughts on standing up to a deal-hungry chairman who saw a company that had
something for three of the companies in his current portfolio (plus
transaction fees on the deal if consummated), my client's being
one of them. This CFO refused to be railroaded into an almost
certainly disastrous acquisition. "It was the most screwed-up
company I have ever seen in my whole life. The company didn't
even have financials. It was running on vapor; all they knew was
they were running through cash pretty quick and they couldn't
even put anything in summary form."

The CFO told the CEO, "Why are we even wasting our time? This thing is a complete train wreck. The CEO responded, "Because the chairman of the board wants to do it. We have to be careful." The CFO was aware of his troubled feelings and was also sensitive to the position of the CEO. Because of his awareness, he could then fashion a method to solve the problem with tact. He agreed to a trip to Europe to review the financials. He told the European company, "Here's what you did last year, here's what you're doing now, and there's a big difference. You are not performing." He requested a detailed plan (which he called a bridge) as to "how to get from where we are to where we are going to be for each of your product groups."

> I set it up that for each of the businesses they had to give me a bridge from where they were to where they expected to be, and where the operational issues that had to be executed were going to be in order to produce the numbers they proffered. What activities are involved to produce these results? We had a meeting of a cast of thousands; we had at least fifty people from [our company] and they had a whole entourage. It became pretty obvious to everybody as they were going through the bridges that there was no way they could do it. It was fiction. I didn't have to say anything. We had cocktails and a meal with the prospective acquisition. That was the only way we could have an intelligent conversation, and I let them tell on themselves.

As explained in this chapter, psychological autonomy permits an awareness of your values, motives, and internal conflicts as well as of the pressures of the outside environment, ideally without allowing either internal or external demands to govern your decisions. You must have a strong core personality to maintain a relative autonomy from your inner drives and outside influences.

7

Integrative Capacity
Seeing Reality with Both Eyes Open

Integrate what you believe in every single area of your life. Take your heart to work and ask the most and best of everybody else, too.

— MERYL STREEP

INTEGRATIVE CAPACITY IS the third of the four elements of active coping. It requires many of the same qualities as psychological autonomy and then takes the process a step further. By integrative capacity I mean not just perceiving and balancing inner and outer pressures but processing the incoming information to create an increasingly complex framework of understanding. The first requirement of integrative capacity is to perceive the world around you clearly, as well as the world inside of you. The second part is to tolerate what you observe without denial or a selective "pick-and-choose" outlook. The third part is to comprehend what you have observed: to see patterns, make connections, and absorb the information, integrating your perceptions into your mental structure. As you might imagine, leaders who possess this mental flexibility are better able to assess problems and find workable solutions than those who do not. Though many individuals can assess problems, those with integrative capacity can both assess problems and resolve them.

Integrative capacity requires complex thought, but it goes beyond sheer intelligence. Pure cognitive ability does not supply the psychic resilience and cohesion required to engage in open and synthetic thinking. Leaders, to be effective, must also have the strength of character to be open to awareness of their own feelings and those of others. They must have the capacity for empathy. In this sense, an integrative capacity resembles many of the qualities of psychological autonomy and integrity.

Any useful theory of leadership is based on the premise that an effective leader fulfills some of the needs of the group by helping its members manage their internal and external environments.[1] Leaders are more likely to be able to meet these needs if they can sense and understand what the group's members want and what motivates them. That ability is stronger in leaders who have more integrative capacity. It is a pure correlation.

We expect effective leaders to show sensitivity to and awareness of the feelings and attitudes of those around them. In support of this view, a study on emergent leaders showed that from 48 to 82 percent of the variance in leadership ratings could be explained by a stable personality attribute described as "the ability to perceive the needs and goals of a constituency and adjust one's personal approach to group action accordingly."[2]

The authors of that study concluded that individuals who emerge as small group leaders develop acuity in anticipating the needs of their followers and change their own behaviors to respond more effectively to those needs. Group members are more willing to follow the person who responds to them, helping them achieve their needs and avoid frustration. Such a person emerges as the leader, who is understood by the sociologist Georg Simmel as being the embodiment of the group's will. The leader does not dictate behavior but becomes the means for the group to achieve its collective goals.

Remember the three levels of psychological functioning: conscious, semiconscious, and unconscious. Like integrity, integrative capacity operates across these levels. It also involves the coordination of behaviors across various psychological functions—cognitive, emotional, interpersonal, and fantasy. What happens "inside" leaders is as important as what they do on the outside. Effective leaders maintain a balance between their internal needs and the challenges, threats, and opportunities they face in the workplace.

Few leaders have been handed a tougher balancing act than Abraham Lincoln. He was elected to run a government, and a country, broken into factions that ranged from staunchly proslavery and states' rights to rigidly abolitionist. He came into a power structure in Washington full of smart, determined men with more experience and social acumen than he. Despite his position as president, he could not force the government to support the changes he wished to achieve. He had to get the measure of these men and choose carefully when and how to act in order to create lasting change in America's laws and society. Although Lincoln's initial goal was to reunify the country, historians have debated this singular goal and questioned whether abolishing slavery was another of Lincoln's goals. Lincoln wrote, "I am naturally anti-slavery. If slavery is not wrong, nothing is wrong. I cannot remember when I did not so think, and feel."[3]

The start of the Civil War gave Lincoln an opportunity to circumvent what was perceived as legal support for states' rights. As commander-in-chief, he could suspend normal operations of civil law but could not emancipate the slaves by fiat. Some of his generals, including McClellan, opposed abolition, and in the middle of a war with no certain outcome, they held great power over Lincoln. He had to craft an argument that would leave them no room for dissent.

Lincoln eventually convinced many nonabolitionists in the government to support emancipation by arguing that emancipation was a necessary act of war. Slaves were helping the South win battle after battle by doing work required to support the fighting—digging trenches, cooking meals, tending to the wounded—enabling the Confederate soldiers to do nothing but fight. The Union soldiers lacked that advantage. Lincoln used this argument in a draft of the Emancipation Proclamation, which he read to his cabinet on July 22, 1862. He warned of his intention to decree the freeing of slaves as a "fit and necessary war measure for suppressing" the Confederate forces. But it was months before he could find the opportune moment to enact it. He waited until the marginal victory at Antietam on September 17, 1862, gave him the psychological high ground both to publish the Emancipation Proclamation on September 22, 1862[4] and eventually to remove the vacillating McClellan and replace him with Ulysses S. Grant.

The Thirteenth Amendment to the U.S. Constitution abolished slavery and involuntary servitude, excluding punishment for a crime. The Senate passed it on April 8, 1864, and the House on January 31, 1865, with much political intervention by Lincoln to secure the necessary votes. Lincoln was assassinated in April 1865, but the movement continued. Secretary of State William H. Seward announced the Thirteenth Amendment to have been adopted by the requisite number of states on December 18, 1865.

Lincoln's path to the unification of the country, the Emancipation Proclamation, and the Thirteenth Amendment is an example of integrative capacity. Many times the political, judicial, and military will was against abolitionism. But Lincoln's intention was not to force through emancipation at all costs. Rather, he waited until he had the political and social forces that would enable him to do so. He had to act with force and careful regard for the feelings of his cabinet, the military, blacks, and the country at large.

Integrative Capacity in Executives—Making All Roads Lead to Rome

Integrative capacity is a significant determinant of effectiveness in executives. Like presidents and generals, executives must take in, analyze, and make decisions based on large amounts of information from many sources every day. An eminent lawyer stated:

> We filter down a situation to the issues on our biggest assignments. We solve [the problem] by showing the good data to the decision makers, and it's not always a happy ending. Sometimes it's, "How much do you pay to get out of a bad decision?" Every time [our practice group] has done these major mediations, we have done the analysis. Our ability is to show somebody that this is the right path because we have analyzed it five ways to hell, and we can make the case that this is why it is the right thing to do. The key to that is really finding the truth, finding what is going to trip you up on the other side and looking at it in the mirror and admitting it.

This statement illustrates intellectual empathy. It shows integrative capacity in seeing the various positions and integrating the factors to make a final decision.

The executives in the next section demonstrate the difference between a person who cannot look in the mirror and find the truth and one who can.

Cynthia Versus Jim

Cynthia was an up-and-coming operating executive. She had pulled herself up by sheer determination out of an impoverished background into a position running a division of a multi-billion-dollar company that had recently been spun out of a Fortune 500 company. She had begun her career at that company and had advanced within the ranks as a result of her intelligence and drive.

Cynthia had been such a superstar at her company that my client was considering her to succeed him as CEO of a multi-billion-dollar company that was a supplier to Cynthia's company.

In certain positions, with the right support structure, she *was* highly effective. But she was *not* qualified to be CEO, where she would be the final decision maker as well as the public face of the company. Here, her poor judgment and abrasive personality would have come to the fore. My assessment pinpointed those weaknesses, and my client rejected her candidacy.

Shortly after my client rejected her, she was snapped up to lead a billion-dollar division of yet another Fortune 500 firm. Less than a year later, the board decided the organization would be better off without her and replaced her. This fact was reported to me by two independent sources, one of them a board member, the other an industry insider. They both cited her domineering and critical style and the ill will she engendered. That ended her ascent in the industry. She has remained in middle management ever since.

Cynthia is among the smartest executives I have ever assessed. Temperamentally energetic and extroverted, she is extremely persuasive and relentlessly driven. She comes across as self-assured and self-confident. Throughout her career, she has relied on her intelligence and sheer force of will to defend against and compensate for aspects of her personality she finds too shameful to admit (such as her depression). She avoids painful feelings while managing relationships so that coworkers are forced to bear the brunt of what she refuses to accept in herself. She does not connect with people in a human, intimate way. She has no friends and no concept of reciprocity or give and take. She sees coworkers as potential rivals or imagined adversaries. She imparts no sense of shared undertaking or community.

Like most other executives, Cynthia pursues leadership primarily to get power over others. But deep down, she sought power because she feels herself to be powerless, a victim. She cannot tolerate this state of helplessness. She is not just very competitive; to win she reflexively reacts in a way that others would view as immoral. When her power is threatened, she reacts without thinking to assert her dominance. That is why past and potential colleagues feel obliquely put down when they meet with her.

Had that been the only problem created by her style, she might have continued along her high-powered career trajectory, but she has another problem. To suppress her inner preoccupations, she acts without thinking through their effect on others demonstrating the opposite of integrative capacity. Her reflexive need to take action suppresses her empathy. In addition, because she needs action for action's sake, she is unable to think through important strategic considerations that other executives of her rank would find obvious.

Executives like Cynthia are not uncommon. They assert dominance and control over others as a way to reverse their own sense of powerlessness. Their energy is alluring at first, but sooner or later their lack of emotional openness begins to repel rather than attract. When you meet this type of person, you feel a negative vibe. They may initially impress—but in a way that makes you doubt yourself. You probably won't be able to identify what turns you off until after you have spent time working with such a person.

Uncovering this sort of behavior during the hiring process is difficult, unless the person hiring has some idea what to look for, as my client did after hearing my report. Former employers will likely have signed covenants not to sue or malign her as a way to protect both parties from future damage. Also, no one likes to admit to feeling devalued or enraged, which are all too often byproducts of encounters with a person like Cynthia. But eventually, executives of this sort will find they have alienated all of their contacts and cannot get good references or other help from others in their careers.

I suggested that my client interview those who provided references and others in the industry with whom she had worked more carefully, particularly in the areas of interpersonal relations and judgment. In doing so, my client discovered that many of her colleagues were bruised by her blunt, ruthless pursuit of power and that she would probably not be effective CEO.

What is it about Cynthia's coping style that caused her to ruin her future prospects like this? She was a passive coper, as defined in chapter 1 and described further in chapters 3 and 4. Chapter 4 explained the use of projective storytelling techniques to reveal underlying passivity in apparently active executives and showed how that covert passivity could go undiscovered until put under great stress, surfacing at the worst possible time. Chapter 1 also gave examples of some famous historical figures who were exceptional active copers under the right circumstances but who also exhibited passive coping at inopportune moments in their careers, much like Cynthia. Unlike Cynthia, these historical figures were generally active copers with holes in their egos. Cynthia most closely resembles Hemingway in putting on a façade of courage but who at an unconscious level was deeply conflicted about his manhood but kept his conflict hidden from himself and most others through his hypermasculine posturing. Both Cynthia and Hemingway were passive copers systemically, not episodically, unlike Churchill and Grant.

Cynthia is a textbook example of a brilliantly successful passive coper who flamed out in her career. When she rose to a position that required more unfiltered interaction with peers and superiors, her lack of authenticity manifested itself and led to greatly dysfunctional relationships. Her inability to relate emotionally to colleagues disqualified her as a candidate for CEO. Her effectiveness at a higher level would depend on functional relationships with colleagues and subordinates, relationships she could not maintain.

To summarize, Cynthia's constant activity was not active coping; it was the opposite. She used it to block out aspects of her humanity (feelings of doubt, insecurity) in order to feel that she was not a victim. Her readiness to take charge was not leadership. Rather, it was a compulsion to dominate that caused others to resist. She was driven by her insecurities. The projective storytelling technique revealed underlying depression and a negative self-image that she defended against through denial and counteraction (her hyperaggressive, energetic, charismatic surface style).

Cynthia's need to take action was a defense that served to keep her unaware of painful childhood experiences she reported to me in the assessment. In addition, she was quite willing to act against the interests of the whole when the action served to keep her unaware of her own feelings. In fact, her psychological cohesiveness depended on cutting off aspects of her emotional experience.

This weakness—this lack of openness to most aspects of her internal world—would sabotage her career no matter how hard she works on external problems. Being closed off to her inner world makes her less able to read and connect with what is going on outside her. She blunders ahead, blind to the nuances of relationships and the complexities of situations. What passes for surface activity in Cynthia masks an underlying passivity. This flaw is built into her psychological structure and is thus unlikely to change.

Cynthia is a real person. She is also a good example of an executive whose flaws are not as visible or damaging earlier in her career, when, had she been made aware of them, she could have done something about them. By the time she rose to be seriously considered as a candidate to be CEO of a Fortune 500 company, she had already deeply offended too many peers who might have otherwise been willing to hire her or support her candidacy. An in-depth assessment earlier in her career could have predicted her self-destructive tendencies. With professional support and sufficient effort of will, she might have learned how colleagues experienced her. She might have developed more empathy and a sense of mutuality if she had been consciously aware of how hurtful it was to feel devalued and abused. Unfortunately, she had defended herself from such insights for too many years to arrive at them on her own. Only long-term insight-oriented therapy would have helped her truly see and own these characteristics in herself.

There are many ways to succeed and many reasons to rise in an organization. In Cynthia's case, the way she treated people blocked her career arc. We will never know if she would have been an effective CEO. Her judgments might not have been wrong, just self-destructive. Cynthia is a clear case of compromised integrative capacity.

An excellent contrast to Cynthia is an executive involved in global private equity with whom I have worked for many years. He is familiar with the evolution of my theory and perceives the complexity of his fiduciary responsibilities, his feelings and motives, and the interpersonal, operational, and financial complexities that surround him, and he does not block out the perception of threats. The following statement by him is an outstanding example of strong integrative capacity:

> When restructuring a company, you generally develop a velocity and an approach as to how you are going to handle the restructuring conceptually. When you step back and look at all the constituencies with regard to the company, you obviously have the labor to the company, management as well as hourly; you have suppliers to the company; you have customers to the company; you have creditors and secured creditors that have lien rights.
>
> Typically you get into trouble because you can't pay the bank back and the bank has taken action to take away your franchise. The knee-jerk reaction is, "What am I going to do with the bank?" What I found is that I have to think in terms of *what part every constituent is going to play in restoring this company to health*. All of the constituencies have to share in the pain; nobody is exempt.
>
> So then you begin to craft how that pain is going to be distributed. There is the usual requirement for additional cash to come from somewhere and it is better, particularly if you are representing the owner, that the additional cash come from the owner or the private equity firm because that becomes a big

leverage item in the negotiation with the other constituents. You then go to the customer and say, "We've got this problem, not the least of which is probably because volumes are down," for example in the auto industry. "We need more money from you and need it in two parts. We need it in a certain amount of liquidity that has to be provided in the form of a loan or an advance and second we need to improve our profitability. I am not selling enough to you at the price we agreed to because I can't cover my fixed expenses so I need price increases." You go to labor and say, "We have too many people and we are paying them too much based upon the revenue stream we've got, so obviously we are going to have to have a discussion about how you are going to take less and how there's going to be fewer people involved." Then you go to the supply base and you have to tell them, "I need longer terms and cheaper prices—a combination of the two—and you need to have patience with me."

Lastly, I can't pay the creditor 100 cents on the dollar. Maybe he reduces the amount that I owe to him. The compelling argument to him is, "If you put us into bankruptcy, you get 10 cents on the dollar. What I am suggesting is that you haircut the amount we owe you by 50 cents on the dollar." If we are able to stay in business, we are able to maintain the service of that debt at a reduced amount. Then the negotiation comes in; how much ownership of the company am I willing to give you so you get the upside of the plan.

It's like juggling all these balls, but everybody has to be willing to cooperate because if anybody moves he pushes it over the side. It's maintaining the equilibrium among all the constituencies. Once you have all the things that you think are possible to be done with the constituencies, you can actually put a restructuring plan together that you think is workable with these concessions.

Integrative capacity comes into play when one's mind is going down five or six different paths and each path is changing. Every time one of them changes, one has to revisit it.

Cynthia's lack of integrative capacity ruined her potential to rise further in the management hierarchy. In contrast, Jim uses his integrative capacity to balance the needs of many competing constituencies, each with its own goals, and finds paths to solvency that all can accept. Like Lincoln, Jim is not afraid to face opposition and setbacks, but he lets his sensitivity to each faction's needs guide him to the least injurious solution and thus to the one most likely to be effective.

A former CEO, we'll call him Mike, at a young age began his management career at his father's company. He related a vivid memory that serves as a metaphor for integrative capacity—seeing reality with both eyes open. His aging father asked him to take over as plant manager for an interim period to restore the company to profitability. The founder/father's office was on the second floor, overlooking the plant floor. The father had painted over the window that would have enabled him to see what occurred on the shop floor.[5] Mike and his father agreed that Mike could take over this office. Mike stripped the paint off the window because he *wanted* to see what was going on in operations. The next day, the workers repainted the window. Mike once again took off the paint and explained to both his father and the workers that in order to be effective in his job, it was necessary to be able to view the shop floor. Mike's direct confrontation of issues was a change in management style, and the "window" became a symbol for everyone in the organization of a more open style of leadership, quite the contrast to that of his father who had built the organization into a successful and, until Mike's brother took over, profitable business.

Mike tells another story, occurring much later in his career, illustrating integrative capacity that vividly demonstrates the relationship between integrative capacity and leadership effectiveness. He was responsible for integrating an acquisition that was twice the size of the acquirer. In addition, he had to contend with eight different labor unions within this acquisition. He discovered during preacquisition due diligence that the company considered its monthly newsletter very effective in communicating with its employees. Mike found, from talking to the people on the plant floor, that no one read the newsletter. The plant employees got their information from their union leadership. This information, in turn, was inconsistent and unreliable.

After the acquisition was completed, Mike explained that real communication cannot occur in a newsletter. It occurs "eyeball to eyeball" so that information can be provided, questions can be asked, and explanations can be given. Mike instituted a new method of communicating with employees. He held a "stand-up" meeting every morning in a different location in this large operation. The union and management leaders were invited, as were any employees who had issues that they felt were important. In a half an hour or less, the management and the employees, including the union leaders, got the chance to communicate information to one another and listen to issues of mutual importance (delivery, safety, quality, and the work environment). It became clear that problems could be solved if they were surfaced and discussed. It was not necessary to use the grievance procedure. The role of the union leadership changed to mutual-gains problem solving. This opened the door to a monthly plantwide discussion of the profit performance of each of the business units. Once the employees on the plant floor and the business unit leaders saw the performance of their business units and the things that contributed to the profit, they began to focus on changes that needed to be made. It became clear that their job security was tied to the profit performance of their business unit. This plant had evolved from a traditional labor-management relationship to one of collaborative problem solving based on mutual respect and real communications.

In this example, Mike demonstrates integrative capacity in bringing together the thoughts and feelings of the workers and their union leaders with management's knowledge of the financials related to the business unit. Workers could communicate directly with Mike and his team and did not need to use the union leadership. He gave the union leadership an opportunity to refocus their efforts. An alliance was achieved among management (Mike), the divisional managers whom the company called business unit leaders, the union leaders, and shop floor workers. Now the unions had an affirmative influence on how the business was run. As this example given by Mike shows, the greater the depth and complexity of a leader's understanding of a situation, the greater his likelihood of achieving a successful resolution.

"Emotional intelligence" has been popular in the literature on leadership. This concept, however, is based on conscious awareness of one's feelings and conscious perceptions of those around one. The construct of active coping includes conscious awareness but extends to include unconscious awareness and a capacity to integrate complexity across conscious and unconscious levels of the personality. Individuals who commit fraud on a recurrent, escalating basis possess high emotional intelligence: they can sense a prospective pawn. Emotional intelligence may be a component of integrative capacity, an awareness of the needs and feelings of others, but only at the conscious level, and it has nothing to do with integrity.

Integrative capacity is a sign of mental health. It, like the other elements of active coping, is constantly in use. It takes stamina and persistence continuously to absorb new and potentially threatening information about yourself and the world around you, analyze it, sort it, and readjust your thinking accordingly. Like the flexibility of an acrobat or a dancer, this mental flexibility requires great energy and will fade if not used regularly.

The persistence that drives integrative capacity also supports the next and final element of active coping. It is not enough to see the way forward; leaders must blaze the trail and have the confidence to stay the course no matter what difficulties arise. They must have sustained power and drive to overcome obstacles and inspire their followers to move forward with them. Channeling this power and drive into constructive achievement rather than giving up is the definition of catalytic coping, the final element of active coping. Catalytic coping is the subject of the next chapter.

8

Catalytic Coping

From this day forward, Flight Control will be known by two
words: "Tough" and "Competent."

—GENE KRANZ, *FAILURE IS NOT AN OPTION*

CATALYTIC COPING, the fourth element of the active coping
style, is the easiest to observe because it comprises both planning and the execution of the plan. It is creativity and activity in
support of a goal. Catalytic coping is a desirable trait in anyone
and an essential trait in leaders. Not only does it enable them to
overcome obstacles to the group's goals, but it also demonstrates
a confidence that inspires and mobilizes their followers. Leadership is as much about actions as words; leaders who accomplish
what they set out to achieve build trust among their followers and
superiors. Their actions continuously communicate their intentions, their competence, their energy, and their determination to
all observers.

Another way to view catalytic coping is the cognitive and behavioral preparedness to transcend problems and implement strategies to achieve distant goals. The problems that leaders encounter
are often not easy to solve. A willingness to persevere when faced
with adversity is a basic requirement for any leader. Proper timing
and the readiness to act at crucial moments are also hallmarks

of effective leaders. Both qualities relate to the ability to steadily pursue long-term goals.

Consider Gene Kranz, the NASA flight director famous for overseeing the safe return of the crippled Apollo 13 mission.[1] Kranz was highly experienced with all aspects of the space program in general and the Apollo program specifically, having written the majority of the "Go/NoGo" and safety procedures himself.[2]

Kranz was also no stranger to catastrophic failures in the space program, having been flight director for the infamous Apollo 1 mission, which ended on the launch pad with a fire killing all three astronauts (Gus Grissom, Ed White, and Roger Chaffee) before they left the ground. Kranz's effective response to the Apollo 1 disaster showed how honestly and openly he faced the terrible mistakes that had been made in the Apollo 1 mission, of which he was flight director, and that he understood and learned from those errors.

Indeed, three days after the incident, he publicly analyzed and admitted the mistakes that had been made in Apollo 1. His address to his branch and flight control team came to be known as the Kranz Dictum:

> Spaceflight will never tolerate carelessness, incapacity, and neglect. Somewhere, somehow, we screwed up. It could have been in design, build, or test. Whatever it was, we should have caught it. We were too gung ho about the schedule, and we blocked out all of the problems we saw each day in our work. Every element of the program was in trouble, and so were we. The simulators were not working, Mission Control was behind in virtually every area, and the flight and test procedures changed daily. Nothing we did had any shelf life. Not one of us stood up and said, "Dammit, stop!" I don't know what Thompson's committee will find as the cause, but I know what I find. We are the cause! We were not ready! We did not do our job. We were rolling the dice, hoping that things would come together

by launch day, when in our hearts we knew it would take a miracle. We were pushing the schedule and betting that the Cape would slip before we did. From this day forward, Flight Control will be known by two words: "Tough" and "Competent." Tough means we are forever accountable for what we do or what we fail to do. We will never again compromise our responsibilities. Every time we walk into Mission Control we will know what we stand for. Competent means we will never take anything for granted. We will never be found short in our knowledge and in our skills.

In the Kranz Dictum, Kranz showed a remarkable ability to analyze and understand honestly and intelligently—and to announce publicly—the errors that had been made in preparing for the launch Apollo 1. The following four Apollo missions were completed without a serious problem. Kranz was the flight director for each of these missions. But nothing is perfect.

Apollo 13 was the third planned lunar-landing mission, launched on April 11, 1970. The first part of the flight went smoothly, but approximately 200,000 miles from Earth an oxygen tank explosion crippled the service and command modules, leaving the crew critically low on oxygen, water, and electrical power.

Once the astronauts reported the extent of the disaster, Gene Kranz and Houston Flight Control sprang into problem-solving mode. They faced problems not covered in any of their written procedures, but they used constant methodical thought and action to imagine, build, test, and document new procedures to keep the spacecraft functional and the astronauts safe.

Kranz's goal during this catastrophe was certainly "distant"; he had to ensure that three men hurtling around the moon got back to Earth alive, despite a damaged ship and critical shortages of oxygen, water, and power. Through rapid problem solving, collaboration, and coordination with the astronauts, Kranz and his team turned what could have been a fatal failure into a heroic victory.

As a leader, Kranz was the epitome of catalytic coping. Although the title of his book, *Failure Is Not an Option*, was actually created for the movie *Apollo 13*, it exemplifies Kranz and the Mission Control mindset. No matter what went wrong, they continued to create, test, and apply solutions. But this was only one side of their strength. Snatching victory from the jaws of defeat makes an interesting story, but like most good leaders, Kranz preferred thorough planning and perfect execution over breathless last-minute solutions. What made Kranz and Mission Control so proficient was their ability both to implement long-term strategies and to respond efficiently to emergencies.

Grant and McClellan: Catalytic Coping in the Civil War

The contrast between the military leadership of Grant and McClellan gives another penetrating view of catalytic coping.

As suggested in chapter 2, McClellan could plan and execute well under peacetime conditions—his army during the early stages of the Civil War was well trained and supplied and his men highly loyal—but McClellan's catalytic coping fell apart under the pressures of war. When McClellan's army was bloodied in battle, he would retreat to a safe place, regroup, replenish, and retrain until he deemed his army ready. This usually took months, until finally an exasperated Lincoln would order him to move. McClellan avoided decisive action by hiding behind indecisive action.

In marked comparison, Grant was a master of catalytic coping. When Grant's army was damaged, he took stock of the situation, learned from the experience, and immediately attacked along a new and more productive line. McClellan constantly thought he was outnumbered—which he never remotely was.[3] He always said he didn't have enough men, fresh horses, or barrels of flour to advance. Grant always believed he could win with whatever he was given. Grant's effectiveness emerged from his own overarching belief that the Union forces would prevail. He refused to entertain the slightest thought that the Union forces might lose the war. Jean Edward Smith says in his biography of Grant: "A general imparts an attitude to an army. It is not simply a matter of issuing orders, but infusing spirit and initiative. An inchoate bond develops between a successful commander and the army. His will becomes theirs."[4] This nonverbal communication is a manifestation of the leader's active coping in generating group effectiveness.

Critics often characterize Grant as a drunk, a straightforward plodder, and butcher of men. In his earlier life he had been a drunk, and he occasionally overindulged during the war, but this was never a factor in a single Civil War engagement.[5] He was, when not constrained by presidential orders or political circumstances, a master of maneuver and one of the architects of the principles of modern war. He was the first general to see victory in war as the result of a series of skirmishes and battles and not necessarily as the result of one or two decisive battles. Grant's greatest and most creative achievement was the Vicksburg campaign, which is one of the most brilliant, long-running campaigns of maneuver in military history.

Campaigning with Grant is a first-person memoir by Grant's aide, Horace Porter.[6] It begins with Grant arriving in Chattanooga in 1864 to take command of a Union army that had just suffered a terrible and surprising defeat at Chickamauga and was almost totally surrounded in difficult terrain by a dangerous and triumphant Confederate force.

Grant was tired from travel, but he sat on a wooden chair in his muddy uniform and listened for an hour as his new subordinates described the apparently hopeless situation. Then he calmly began writing orders—securing the army's supply line and shifting its defenses toward the eventual offensive that would shatter the Confederate besiegers. It was a brilliant and charismatic performance.

Grant made mistakes during the war. Every general did, and some of Grant's were big. But in war, unlike other situations, he was never disheartened or derailed by failure.[7] A memorable and characteristic moment came at the end of the first day of the Battle of Shiloh (1862), in which the Confederates had taken Grant and his men by surprise and mopped up the field with them. As darkness fell and the weary armies licked their wounds before resuming the fight in the morning, General William T. Sherman, Grant's subordinate, rode up to him.

"Well, we've had the devil's own day, haven't we, Grant?" Sherman said.

"Yep," said Grant, chewing on a cigar and quietly surveying the field. "Lick 'em tomorrow, though."[8]

And he did.

No leader ever feels that he has enough horses, men, or barrels of flour. It's his readiness to engage despite obstacles that demonstrates catalytic coping.

Grant illustrates catalytic coping in another sense. His logistical planning was always purpose driven. He "brought every available soldier to the field, sublimating those secondary considerations that so often consumed the attention and resources of weaker generals."[9] He assessed the strengths and weaknesses of Confederate generals who opposed him, and, always a risk taker, he took bolder risks where he sensed indecision or weakness. Jean Edward Smith, in his biography of Grant, says that the "whole campaign against Forts Henry and Donelson seemed a marvel of generalship, a superb combination of simplicity and determination— in stark contrast to the dilatory maneuvering of the forces of Major General Don Carlos Buell or the Army of the Potomac under McClellan."[10]

He goes on to say—and I find this especially important— "Grant, like few American generals before or since, understood the momentum of warfare. He had a quickness of mind that enabled him to make on-the-spot adjustments. His battles were not elegant set-piece operations—as Scott's textbook victory at Cerro Gordo had been—but unfolded unpredictably as opportunities developed."[11] Grant used his quickness of mind to create plans that could be implemented on the spot.

Failure in a battle never caused Grant to lose sight of the greater objective; he took a long-term view of war. But he took care to make the short term functionally effective. He maintained a balance between his vision and his action. His analysis of battles was typically aggressive—as he was to say later, "both sides seemed as if they had been defeated, and whoever assumed the offensive was sure to win."[12]

Grant and, under him, Sherman initiated a new way of warfare that has resonated ever since. War for them was continuous, not episodic. If you were tired, so was your enemy, and there was no better time to press him. Grant's campaigns of 1864 and 1865 consisted of continuous pressure in all theaters of war from Louisiana to Virginia. And the pressure was not only on the enemy's soldiers but also his means of production and communication.

McClellan had a tin ear for communication and was less than astute about politics. He treated his civilian bosses, including President Lincoln (the chairman, if you will, of his board of directors), with open disdain. Grant, conversely, while rumpled and apparently unsophisticated, was, with Robert E. Lee, a consummate political general. Grant was able to negotiate for a reasonable level of resources.

McClellan is one of the most divisive figures in the Civil War. To this day he has his supporters. The fact is that McClellan *was* masterful at organizing, training, and inspiring armies. There was no federal general more popular among his men, even when his campaigns produced one failure after another. His penchant for stopping after each battle to rest and resupply was not unique; it was common practice among all Civil War generals. But McClellan took it to a dysfunctional extreme. He obsessed over his enemies' movements and overestimated their strength to the point where he and his armies were frozen to the spot. Some have said he exaggerated his figures to give himself an excuse in case of failure, but his biographer, Stephen W. Sears, thinks that McClellan truly believed these wild overestimates. He simply could not bring himself to pull the trigger, looking for opportunities to take the defensive even when on the strategic offensive. As Sears explains, McClellan had a gift for imagining the worst-case scenario until he believed it, then acting in a way that made it come true. McClellan's focus on the worst case suggests a predilection for passive coping. This tendency primed him to capitulate when pressed, to flee from threats, to give up rather than seize an enemy's momentary weakness.

Catalytic Coping in the Twenty-First Century

Although executives don't usually have to worry about their workforce surviving physical attack, they have all of the same organizational responsibilities that generals do. They must balance long-term strategy with short-term tactics, bolster their organizations' strengths and shore up its weaknesses, and be prepared to act when the time is right, or even create the right time, as Grant did when he seized the initiative in battle. This requires not physical courage but strength of mind.

In the section below, Jim, the investor I quoted in chapter 7, discusses the mental fortitude necessary to face down opponents in the boardroom:

> I'd love to be able to author a restructuring plan this way: We have a fifteen-minute meeting, everybody agrees to it, and we are able to execute it. It never happens that way. Here, you get into the gamesmanship of it. It comes down to difficult meetings, difficult discussions, and who is going to blink. You have to be comfortable in your own skin or you can't do it. You don't

have to be mean; you just have to be yourself: You have to be so sure that this is the right thing to do that you can withstand personal attacks as you deliver the message.

In the citation above, Jim references both integrity and psychological autonomy. He continued his explanation: "The courage of your convictions is important because your team is looking for that kind of leadership. You can't hide behind some of your colleagues and let them do the dirty work. *Part of leadership is you, front and center.* You are going to take the first blow, not stick one of your subordinates up there and say, 'That didn't work, now what are we going to do?' "

This quotation is a good example of the persistence, determination, and cognitive and behavioral activity that catalytic coping requires as well as the interrelations among the elements of active coping.

I do not view Grant as a paragon of active coping. I use the contrast with McClellan merely to illustrate the element of catalytic coping. Grant died impoverished and suffered from depression. When he had adequate support (the presence of his wife and children) and the right circumstances to activate his talent for leadership, he was successful. After the Civil War, he reverted. He unwisely trusted business associates and was something of a naïf when it came to managing his own business and finances. As president, a number of men he appointed to his cabinet and administration turned out to be corrupt. In his unwise reliance on others in business and politics, Grant showed a blind spot or hole in his coping structure.

As I mentioned at the outset of the book, the vast majority of the assessments I've done have been on male executives. So one could then ask: do the findings of this research apply to women? The next chapter will discuss this issue and suggest what additional work is really needed when addressing this question.

9

Implications for Female Leaders

ON JANUARY 1, 2012, Virginia Rometty became the first female CEO of International Business Machines Corp. Articles about her lauded her ability to blend enthusiasm, charisma, clear communication, strategic thinking, and "cool-minded" decision making. But one *New York Times* story placed the emphasis on the role self-confidence may have played in her success.[1]

> Early in her career, Virginia M. Rometty, I.B.M.'s next chief executive, was offered a big job, but she felt she did not have enough experience. So she told the recruiter she needed time to think about it.
>
> That night, her husband asked her, "Do you think a man would have ever answered that question that way?"
>
> "What it taught me was you have to be very confident, even though you're so self-critical inside about what it is you may or may not know," she said at Fortune's Most Powerful Women Summit this month. "And that, to me, leads to taking risks."

Many women face the problem that Virginia Rometty faced in those early years. Leadership requires a certain degree of self-confidence and aggressiveness. On the issue of self-confidence, women are faced with a heads-you-win, tails-I-lose situation. If they do not display confidence and a certain degree of aggressiveness, they are less likely to be chosen as leaders because leaders need to be confident and aggressive. If, however, they do show a high level of self-confidence and aggressiveness, they are also not likely to be chosen because that is not how women are expected to act. We will return to this central issue later in this chapter.

In one of our Booth studies, noted in the preface to this book, we examined an elite group of male and female MBA students selected for participation in a then-new leadership education and development program. In this study,[2] we came to the conclusion, consistent with the findings of most organizational studies, that the overall difference in the evaluations of male and female leadership effectiveness was negligible. Indeed, women in leadership positions tended to be judged as slightly more effective leaders, overall, as rated by both genders. It is not surprising that a naturalistic setting in which social class and level of education were controlled, female leadership was considered as effective, overall, as male leadership.

Even in this specific group, however, the men and women showed significant differences in leadership style that resembled and seemed to confirm stereotypically gender-linked motives and values. Women scored higher on the communal factor (showing high levels of the desire to affiliate with others, playfulness, tendencies to both nurture and be nurtured by others, and openness to aesthetic experiences) and men scored higher on the agentic factor (exhibiting high levels of dominance, aggression, and exhibitionism).

Reviewers frequently attribute statistically significant correlations showing gender role stereotypes to the researchers' failure to control for social class and education; one might have expected the differences we found to be less pronounced because our study controlled for those factors. But our study also found that exhibiting strong agentic orientations was a negative factor in judgments of women's leadership effectiveness, whereas exhibiting a communal orientation did not create a disadvantage for men.[3]

These gender differences appear to play a crucial mediating role in shaping the judgments of particular male and female leaders. The effect is that women must be stronger copers to overcome bias based on gender stereotypes. Let me expand on this statement.

Our findings fit in with the general view that, all other factors being equal, men may have more latitude than women to lead in a variety of agentic and communal styles without consequence for how they are judged. Gender role stereotypes appear to affect women more than men in leadership roles. Women who adopt a stereotypically male style get along in management less well than men. The similarity in our study between men and women on measures of leadership, intelligence, social class, and education makes the gender differences in motivation and the differential perceptions of male and female leaders possessing agentic orientations particularly striking.

When applied to leadership, the communal and agentic orientations suggest that female leaders were more interpersonally oriented and collaborative in their leadership styles, whereas male leaders were more task oriented and dominating. These gender-linked aspects of leadership style mirror the distinction between interpersonally oriented and task-oriented leadership that were emphasized in studies published in the 1950s and early 1960s.[4] In those studies, called the Ohio State studies, task orientation, labeled *initiation of structure*, included leader behaviors such as having subordinates behave in accord with rules and procedures, making leader and follower roles consistent, and having high standards of performance. Interpersonal orientation, labeled *consideration*, included leader behaviors such as helping and doing favors for followers, looking out for their welfare, explaining procedures, and being friendly and available. Task and interpersonal styles of leadership are not mutually incompatible, but we mostly treat them as separate, relatively orthogonal dimensions.

Our Booth findings suggest that almost forty years after the Ohio State studies women still tended to be negatively judged—indeed, punished—when they exhibited more autocratic, directive leadership styles. Women, if they were to be regarded as effective leaders, were expected to disprove or overcome a negative bias rooted in the belief that the attributes associated with the female gender role are discordant with the agentic qualities that most leaders (who have in the past been men) normally exhibit. This prejudice is probably less strong today as more women, like Virginia Rometty, although still a minority, have moved into top echelons in business corporations and politics.

As mentioned above, men are free to exhibit traditionally agentic or communal styles when leading. In some respects, continuing stereotypically communal styles may help women aspiring to leadership roles because they serve to demonstrate women's group-oriented motivation and their lack of self-oriented motivation in a leadership situation. It is possible that such proof of acceptable motivation may be a prerequisite for effective leadership by women. Men, by contrast, because group members perceived them as having an inherent right to lead, were not suspected of having self-aggrandizing motives and were not required to prove their group-oriented motivation. The ability of communal leadership styles to soften female leaders' potential role conflict may stem from the specific meaning these styles convey. This meaning could be that a leader is concerned about the success of the group, not about enhancing personal power and status.

In the research study, the assumption that leaders from either gender would have to demonstrate task competency to be perceived as effective leaders was supported by our findings. For men and women alike, an active coping style was significantly correlated with leadership. The correlation between leadership effectiveness and overall active coping was higher for women than it was for men.

Nevertheless, we found certain gender differences in coping style (as measured by semiprojective measures of coping) and leadership. For one, for women but not for men, evaluations of leadership were positively and significantly correlated with scores on a measure of the readiness to articulate clearly sources of frustration and difficulties in terms of people, things, and events in the external environment. In addition, for women but not for men, a measure of defensive vagueness and ambiguity was negatively and significantly correlated with leadership effectiveness. Moreover, for women but not for men, a measure of self-confidence and self-esteem was significantly correlated with leadership. Finally, for women but not for men the correlation between leadership effectiveness and the tendency to be invested in impersonal objects and activities (linked to task orientation) was marginally significant.

It appears that female leaders may have been judged according to criteria that were not used to judge male leaders' behaviors. The most effective female leaders appeared to be focused on technical problems and difficulties in the external world. That effective female leaders were especially concerned with technical tasks may reflect a theory about women having to perform extremely well to succeed as managers.

The constraints on women's leadership style raise an important issue: Once women are actually in leadership roles, are women perceived less favorably than men when performing leadership or managerial tasks even though their performance equals that of the men, or is their performance really less effective than those of the men? Our study did not examine that issue. If individuals in business exhibit a bias to judge the efforts of female leaders who display agentic styles less favorably than male leaders' equivalent efforts, women who aspire to leadership roles would encounter serious barriers to entering these roles and advancing to higher levels within an organization. To the extent that our findings can be generalized to organizational settings, they suggest that female managers may be victims of unfair judgments. As women enter male-dominated leadership roles, in organizations in which autocratic styles are common, they may encounter significant bias given the evidence of selective devaluation in our study and others.

To the extent that women either avoid male-dominated leadership roles or else favor an autocratic and directive style, the selective devaluation phenomenon demonstrated in our study would serve to preserve the traditional division of labor and discourage women from seeking or attaining positions of leadership. Our findings indicate that female leaders capable of overcoming the limitations on leadership style must be more self-confident, more task focused, and more open to the perception of frustration and difficulty than their male counterparts. The blend of enthusiasm, charisma, clarity of communication, and strategic thinking for which Virginia Rometty has been praised in the twenty-first century is consistent with these findings.

To be an effective leader, it is important to be able to strike an appropriate balance between assertiveness and cooperation. Ideally, both male and female leaders will choose their actions sensibly and flexibly depending on the situations they confront. Expressive, relationship-oriented behaviors such as consideration of others, playfulness, and emotional expressiveness are traditionally feminine characteristics that contribute to high morale and cohesiveness in small task groups. Our findings suggest that men and women alike expect women to serve these functions in the workplace, but these functions are also appreciated when they appear in men—they are not viewed as "effeminate." Independence, decisiveness, and ambition also are requisites of effective leadership. Yet it appears that women are not allowed to display these qualities if they are to succeed as leaders. Given the conflicts, impediments, and disadvantageous stereotypes imposed on women in leadership roles, it is not surprising that women have to be stronger copers than men to establish legitimacy and credibility as leaders. As a whole, these findings indicate that women have to have high self-esteem and high self-confidence while leading in a communal style in order to be perceived as effective leaders. In short, they must be stronger copers in order to transcend the constraints placed on their leadership style.

PART II

Enhancing Your Active Coping

10

Past Is Not Necessarily Prologue
Improving Your Active Coping

Our ambition should be to rule ourselves, the true kingdom for
each one of us; and true progress is to know more, and be more,
and to do more.

— OSCAR WILDE

THIS CHAPTER and the two that follow focus on how to develop
and strengthen your own coping style. This chapter discusses
general considerations in self-assessment. Chapter 11 provides
a method for assessing oneself with a view to improving one's
coping. Chapter 12 presents an example of a mature, successful
executive who reflected verbally on the elements of active coping
this book describes and discussed how he developed active coping.

Introduction to Self-Assessment

A CEO of a wireless networking and telecommunications company once described himself to me as a "scavenger of good ideas."
This vivid self-characterization captures the information acquisi-
tiveness and resourcefulness that we associate with active coping.
These qualities are also needed to strengthen other qualities that
fall under the rubric of active coping. Some executives develop
active coping on their own, and many have good mentors, spouses,

and friends to help them. But they continue to work on developing their active coping. The second section of this chapter offers a framework and provocative questions for examining one's own psyche and behavior so that one can become more aware of one's strengths and possible areas for improvement.

Active coping is not fixed. It is a term I use for a combination of psychological qualities that make it easier for a person to deal with real-life problems effectively and autonomously. Everything is both cause and effect of the development in which it takes place. This is the essence of dialectical thinking.

Dealing with life's challenges and changes effectively strengthens these underlying qualities, which in turn make it possible to deal still more effectively with problems in the future. Improvement is not infinite. There are limits. Not everyone can alter their coping: passive copers will have trouble even with the best professional help. As I have mentioned several times, we are all shaped by our early history. The deeper levels of behavior are particularly difficult to change. Many of us, however, do have the potential to grow and change, and I would hope that those who possess this potential become more aware of and more at peace with themselves. The more one possesses the elements associated with active coping—integrity, psychological autonomy, integrative capacity, and catalytic coping—the more likely it is that one can continue to develop them.

Tim, the first of the active copers described in chapter 3, showed how as a young adult he managed to change, on his own, his passive into active coping—and became not only wealthy but also led the development of major devices in cancer treatment and now is CEO of a major cancer treatment device company. He had the underlying elements of active coping and the motivation and intelligence to reverse his passive into active coping. As Tim's transformation shows, we can change without the help of a psychotherapist and without a depth psychological assessment by using self-diagnostic tools, a mentor, and/or experiential learning. But we must be honest with ourselves.

The modules that follow the second section in this chapter list some of the questions one might ask oneself to enhance one's active coping and presents a self-help program for developing active coping. Developing active coping takes time, experience, and constant reevaluation. With experience comes awareness, with awareness comes mastery, and with mastery comes the added flexibility and resourcefulness that contribute to greater active coping.

As stated repeatedly throughout this book, the elements of active coping contribute to healthy personality growth and strong performance. They do so by optimizing an individual's responses to specific problems and by fostering continuing psychological richness, self-confidence, and resourcefulness. Success and even failure create a base of experience on which future coping is built if one has the underlying qualities associated with active coping.

Active coping is important for all of us whether or not we occupy positions of power because it allows us to see and respond to reality with our eyes open. As a result, we are more likely to supply the response that is effective. Actually, it involves more than seeing and understanding; it is changing and growing. It is a key to performing consistently well.

General Considerations in Self-Assessment

It is important to understand that all of us bring our personal lives, our past, and our unconscious into the workplace. Often this plays itself out in the phenomenon known as *transference*. Transference is the application to a new situation of old unconscious patterns of relationship—some useful, some not. A boss may remind you of a parent you wanted to please, and so you may work particularly hard to be a star in his or her work group.

Or a colleague may bring to mind a hated classmate, provoking you to unreasonable reactions.

Transference lives on and on, like other repressed phenomena. Transference occurs when one takes one's own perceptions and expectations and projects them onto another person. One then interacts with the other person as if that person *is* the original source of the transference. The transference distorts the reality of the current figure.

In contrast to Tim, who understood that he needed to change when he was still a young adult, let us look at a venture capitalist I'll call Greg. Greg is an example of someone who was much older than Tim and already established as a venture capitalist before he realized that his career was not developing as he had hoped and that he himself might be to blame for that. Before Greg came to me, he had risen to be a partner in a known venture capital firm, but his future there did not look good.

As a venture capitalist, his advice was generally seen to be outstanding, but he delivered his insights in a sarcastic, demeaning, and insulting way. Other venture capitalists hated working with him because of how he made them feel. Greg's abrasive personality made it impossible for him to forge close working relationships. His partners increasingly ignored him, even excluded him from deals. He eventually realized that he needed help if his career were to move forward.

He turned to me as a coach to help him resolve his problems. Over a period of four years of working closely with me, Greg became aware that he denied his partners the same respect and admiration that he craved for himself.

While discussing his childhood, Greg began to see the origins of his disparaging behavior. He had longed for his mother's approval, but she had responded to his vulnerability with sarcasm and derision. This was *exactly* how Greg behaved as an adult. Decades after his childhood, working at a prominent venture capital firm, Greg treated his partners and CEOs of his firm's portfolio companies the same way his mother had treated him. He wanted to be liked and admired but because he feared rejection he belittled others to hide his insecurity.

Eventually Greg understood that he treated his partners and portfolio CEOs poorly because their needs for approval reminded him of his own needs for approval, which threatened him. He was more comfortable being cold, rejecting, and condescending than with letting this vulnerability show. His abrasiveness undermined him even though it was unconsciously intended to protect him. He needed the safety of our relationship to have this insight.

Once Greg came to this realization, he became more accepting of his needs. His desire for approval was no longer as great a threat to his psychological security. He was more able to give praise to his partners, to compliment and congratulate them, and to make tradeoffs and compromises. He became a warmer, more engaging person. Other venture capitalists now seek him out, and his career has resumed an upward trajectory.

Greg had unresolved unconscious conflicts with authority figures and peers that compromised his ability to trust others. At work, he behaved defensively rather than openly. His transference to authority figures got in the way of his ability to establish collaborative and productive relationships.

As Greg's experience indicates, people who are able to nurture others and allow others to nurture them tend to be more productive and are better liked by their colleagues. Too often, work creates a tension between doing your job well and being attentive to and nurturing human connections. Doing your job well may mean leaving others behind or making unpopular decisions. Psychological autonomy, an element of active coping, helps you to make peace with this tension—for example, not allowing pressure to conform or guilt to cloud your judgment. Integrity helps as well, should the decision involve ethical considerations.

Integrative capacity, closely associated with psychological autonomy and integrity, helps you balance all relevant considerations and resolve the tension. For example, no one likes to fire employees, even if they are underperforming. It takes considerable psychological energy, but once the task is done—and doing the task is catalytic coping—individuals who possess the qualities associated with active coping accept the necessity of their actions. George Washington (showing integrity in the moral sense) did not merely free his slaves. He tried to make sure that they would survive: job training for the young, pensions for the old, jobs for those in between. A business executive will not just fire employees to save money but will do his best to do it as caringly as possible.[1]

Why do some of us have trouble coping in parts of our lives even though it is so important to our careers and happiness? In Greg's case, he didn't know he had a blind spot. He simply didn't have a clue. Greg's predicament is far more common than we realize.

Blind spots, or lack of self-awareness, often stem from *resistance*. Resistance is what keeps us from changing. There are two levels of resistance: The first is resistance to self-awareness. We resist insight because it is painful. It stirs up memories we'd prefer to forget or feelings we'd rather avoid. We defend ourselves by refusing to see aspects of who we are. We deny or disavow them. Or we split them off from conscious awareness but experience them vicariously through others. It was easier for Greg to treat the needs of his coworkers with contempt than to admit he had those same needs. Once he was more comfortable tolerating those needs in himself, he was far more relaxed and effective dealing with the needs of others at work.

We may resist awareness when we are forced to make tradeoffs. For many, the most difficult choice is between work and family. Moving to a new location may conflict with the needs of children and spouses. Making tradeoffs forces us to discover the limits of how much we can achieve. Individuals who have the self-awareness, flexibility, and adaptability associated with active coping accept these limitations and move on.

Some of us change at the moment we develop greater awareness. We may have limitations, but once a deficiency is pointed out, we see and overcome it. Others need to dig deep before finding the strength to change. Greg was like that. Still others gain awareness but are unable to change. Like a Woody Allen character, they will say that they see the issue and intellectually they seem to understand it. But they use their understanding as an evasion, a way of avoiding the feelings involved in actually changing. Often they sabotage their careers by not doing what they know they should do.

This is the second level of resistance I mentioned: resistance to change. We resist change because we develop a style that fits our early experiences and fear breaking out if it. Passive copers run away from awareness. Active copers become stronger because they don't give up or shut down. They use anxiety and discomfort to push themselves toward mastery and growth.

Also, when we see our limitations, we suffer a psychological blow. We realize we are mortal and imperfect. We may work all our lives to achieve positions in which we can move events—and then we discover we can't control them. Active copers are able to tolerate or reframe such disappointments. Here it helps to have a sense of humor and irony. Passive copers can also reframe such disappointments but do not find the means to move on, to create a new path or goal. They simply tolerate the disappointment.

Developing active coping takes time, experience, and constant self-reevaluation. It requires facing the resistance and trying to avoid denial—denial of the reality as it is rather than what one would like it to be. With experience may come awareness, one of the keys to active coping; however, individuals who cope passively at the deeper levels of personality may merely use experience to bolster their own twisted conceptions. Let us consider more deeply the process of developing the qualities of active coping: integrity, psychological autonomy, integrative capacity, and catalytic coping.

Strengthening Each Element of Active Coping

We will begin with integrative capacity, the third element of active coping as presented in this book in chapter 7—the openness to perceive complexity. As stated there, integrative capacity requires many of the qualities of psychological autonomy and then takes the process a step further. Greg learned to integrate an awareness of the world outside him and the world within him, to tolerate that awareness, and to comprehend what he observed, absorbing the information and integrating his perceptions into his mental structure. With respect to developing integrative capacity, the first part involves *awareness of your personal goals as well as opportunities in the environment.* Can you define what it is you want to achieve? Are your goals realistic, or are they grandiose? Are they specific, or are they nebulous? Are they compatible, or do they conflict?

Take the young woman I'll call Caroline. I began working with Caroline after she received a major promotion at her investment bank. She was promoted despite that in countless little ways she had been sabotaging her career. Her superiors clearly recognized that her strengths clearly outweighed her weaknesses.

The promotion threw Caroline into a panic. Not until she identified the discomfort associated with making a success of the promotion did she see how she was sabotaging her career. Once she felt safe enough to talk about and understand what motivated her self-defeating behavior could she resolve her ambivalence about success.

Caroline had achieved a great deal in her career while being unclear about what it was she wanted to achieve. She had worked hard but had avoided taking the initiative. This was possible in the lower-level positions she had occupied till her promotion. Her promotion made her responsible for a significant area in the company and meant that she now had to generate new business and report to a new division head. It was a job she both wanted and feared.

Though pleased with the recognition, she confided to me that in many ways she preferred her former, more subordinate role.

Over the course of our work together, she began to become aware that she had had a complicated relationship with her father growing up. He belittled her achievements while letting her know he expected her to excel. As a result, she developed ambivalence about success. Her ambivalence arose from the fact that her father expected her to excel but that nothing she accomplished seemed to satisfy him. Understandably, she was unable to throw herself into work and take significant risks with the full commitment that success required. As a result, she was worried—more than she first realized—that her work in her new role would disappoint everyone.

This brings us to the second part of integrative capacity: *recognizing sources of threats or frustration*. If you know what you want and what is getting in the way of attaining it, you have a better chance of overcoming that obstacle. Without identifying the threat or obstacle, you depend on luck to make it go away. Caroline was ambivalent about what she wanted. Her goals were unclear. In her case, the source of frustration was internal. She was her own worst enemy. As she came to understand this, she was able substantially to resolve her ambivalence about success. After a time in her new position she was promoted again to a much more independent position running an important area of her firm's investment banking business. She became and remains one of the top investment bankers in her firm.

One of the reasons she became one of the top investment bankers in her firm was that she was put in a position where her little weaknesses didn't matter as much as they might have when she was in a lower position and where her strengths, once she became able to use them, such as her vision, creativity, communication skills, and customer care, came to the fore. Caroline's story shows that overcoming a deficiency in an area associated with active coping depends not only upon awareness of one's inner world (in her case, her profoundly ambivalent feelings about her father and her association of any authority figure with her father); it is also the position one occupies. As mentioned, her bank probably promoted her because her superiors understood that her self-defeating weaknesses in her lower-level positions would not matter as much when she was made responsible for significant areas of business in the organization.

In other cases, the source of frustration may be external. What stands in the way is the real world. You are competing with others who want the same job, and only one person is going to get it. Or family demands keep you from working long hours. Or you bump into a glass ceiling.

How openly, how realistically you perceive problems profoundly influences your chances for success. The best strategies anticipate setbacks, develop options, and prepare you to identify solutions. In *The Art of War* Sun Tzu emphasizes this openness to perceive complexity, including possible future threats. He writes, "In peace prepare for war, in war prepare for peace. The art of war is of vital importance to the state. It is a matter of life and death, a road either to safety or to ruin. Hence under no circumstances can it be neglected."

Some individuals may create myths about themselves. For example, they may be unable to imagine they *could* fail. They'll point to ways they've turned every situation to their advantage rather than admit weakness. Usually such myths mask a deep-seated feeling of having been traumatized early in life. The sense of being special, of having a unique gift, helps counteract the helplessness associated with early trauma.

When we do not acknowledge our fears, we cannot see how much our workplace performance is designed to avoid them. We go through life with one hand tied behind our backs. Many jobs can be performed with one hand. But, as Caroline's story shows, when we rise in our careers, performing well consistently requires both hands. Acknowledging our fears means being honest and articulating what we experience as threatening.

Successful leaders shine because they have the psychological strength that allows them to confront, acknowledge, and overcome sources of frustration so they can move toward their positive goals. To attain a certain status in our careers may unconsciously mean surpassing a parent we were afraid to outshine or rising above those who have mentored us. A long-sought promotion like Caroline's may terrify us once we finally get it because we are forced to confront a conflict that was obscured by being a subordinate.

Even if we learn what we want, reality usually does not immediately gratify our desires. When we pretend that a conflict between what we want and what we can have does not exist, chances are we are coping passively with a part of ourselves. We are cutting off aspects of our humanity. When we try to ignore our desires and passions, we not only make ourselves unhappy; we also are not as successful as we could be. That is why it is important to be aware of our needs as well as the needs and demands of others and the external world that impinge on us—and to have *the psychological freedom to choose how to act*: in other words, the essence of psychological autonomy, the subject of chapter 6 in this book.

Remember George Fisher from the preface to this book? He recognized that he could not transform the culture at Kodak, nor could he bring about the necessary reengineering the company required, so he resigned. He never again became a CEO. He could not overcome his failure at Kodak to attain another position as CEO, even in a company with a culture more reminiscent of the nimble one at Motorola under his tenure. Some executives need to change careers to remain important forces in the business world.

This brings us to catalytic coping, the process of actually *dealing with resistance and overcoming threats*, as opposed to avoiding, withdrawing, or giving up, like George Fisher. How prepared are you to tackle obstacles that may hinder the execution of your plans?

When stressed, do you retreat into yourself or lash out at others? If so, you may fail to motivate and inspire at a time when the need for leadership is greatest.

We feel best about ourselves—we have our highest self-esteem— if we are *pursuing what we really want in a way that is consistent with our values and ideals and those of our community and which we honestly believe are for the moral good of mankind.* This element of active coping relates to integrity. It is important to know what drives us and to reassess our goals as we change and the world around us changes. Knowing what is really most important to us, we are able to commit to pursuing meaningful goals and accept the fact that we may not succeed. We experience confidence if we pursue goals that are realistically within our grasp—but high enough to stretch us.

There is a creative element to active coping. A core aspect of it cannot be taught. Some individuals cannot or will not change. As I have emphasized, active coping is an attribute of personality structure, like character. It is hard to change this structure, even if you can see the basic fault lines. Without a significant basis of active coping, change is even harder.

But even that information can be useful. For example, if you can recognize where you might be passive, you can hire someone else to cover that area for you or steer yourself into areas where you are not going to be passive. When you understand how you cope, your style, and know which situations draw out your vulnerabilities, you can avoid those situations. As Kenneth Blanchard and Spencer Johnson write, "We are not just our behavior. We are the person managing our behavior."[2] Individuals with the psychological qualities associated with active coping have a higher probability of adapting to life's challenges because, as stated early on in this chapter, they have the psychological freedom to choose the response that has the greatest likelihood of a successful outcome, however they define it.

11

Self-Assessment for Strengthening Active Coping

NOW WE COME TO A CONCRETE framework for developing our psychological strength. The personal development/self-assessment modules outlined apply to the desire to develop yourself, whether you are a musician, an artist, a corporate executive, an entrepreneur, or a professional such as a lawyer. I focus on business executives, but the process applies to anyone seeking to gain the openness to perceive and integrate complexities and the ability to carry out or make another plan to achieve one's goals whatever the obstacles may be—all in a fashion consistent with one's values and ideals.

The personal development portion of a self-assessment examines how one responds to stress. To the extent one handles stress in a psychologically healthy manner, one is better able to perceive openly and respond appropriately to reality. Whatever the undertaking or plan (and I am not talking about painting one picture or making one sculpture but rather devoting oneself to a career—and potentially a change of careers—as a sculptor, lawyer, or business executive), you may benefit from knowing how your psyche potentially interferes with or enhances your ability to see opportunities and threats and to address them adaptively, in a way that improves your chances of success.

The four modules I describe build on one another. They address each element of active coping. The outcome should be enhanced emotional capacity to carry out the plan in a successful, confident manner.

I encourage readers to work with someone they trust, someone who may know them better than they know themselves. Many of us have a blind spot—a lack of understanding of our weaknesses or a failure to appreciate our strengths. A friend, mentor, or therapist can help point these out. The person does not have to be a professional psychologist. Good mentors are worth their weight in gold.

Schematic for a Twenty-Week Assessment of Your Coping Style

The following four paragraphs summarize the modules developed for self-assessment and development. They are introductions to the more detailed modules that follow them. At the end of each module is an opportunity to summarize what you have learned and to think about it for the subsequent module, including what you might not be looking at and how that may play out. That might be just what you need to instigate growth.

> Module 1. *Aims and Goals*: What are your (implicit and explicit) goals and values, and is the manner in which you propose to realize them consistent with your current or proposed venture or goal?
>
> Module 2. *Frustrations*: How well do you anticipate contingencies that might threaten the success of the venture or

interfere with achieving the goal? How realistically does your plan address such threats?

Module 3. *Catalytic Coping*: How will you adapt to contingencies that may arise? What may interfere psychologically with the ability to exploit opportunities and overcome threats?

Module 4. *Self-Esteem*: In synthesizing the previous modules, you may better determine whether you want to go forward, and how. You may better understand where your decisions are likely to be good, in what situations they are likely to be weak, and how to optimize the use of your psychological resources.

Give yourself three to four weeks to cover each module. Given four modules, plan to devote fifteen to twenty weeks to complete an honest, comprehensive self-assessment. At the end, you should wind up with an ability to see opportunities and threats more openly and to integrate the perception more effectively, with enhanced self-awareness, psychological autonomy, catalytic coping, and self-esteem.

Module 1: Articulation of Aims and Goals

What are your aims and goals? And why do you want to pursue them? Spend at least one session with each of these areas: professional goals, personal goals, social goals, and overall life goals.

Professional goals: What are your professional goals, short term and long term? Why do you want to pursue them, from an emotional point of view? Let's say, for instance, you are an entrepreneur and want to continue on that path or that you want to become an entrepreneur. Given that, then this analysis is an attempt to understand why it is you wanted or want to start a business. What's the psychological motivation? You have to understand what motivates you, what drives you, so that internal psychological forces don't wind up sabotaging you or making you miserable. Why do you want to be an entrepreneur from a personal point of view? What's the personal meaning of starting a business? What does it mean to you to be an entrepreneur? What do you fantasize as your goals, what motive, what passion do you expect being an entrepreneur will satisfy? The same sets of questions apply to other professional aspirations, whether it's being an artist, a hedge fund manager, or an executive climbing the corporate ladder.

Personal goals: What is your life plan? What are your developmental *plans* for your life? What are the your lifelong aims, not just current or five-year goals but ten, fifteen, twenty years out? You may want to ask yourself, for example, where do I want to be financially? Do I want to travel or volunteer for a cause that has personal meaning? Going back to the example of becoming an entrepreneur, how does starting a new venture fit into your aims over the course of your lifespan? Have you planned sufficiently for retirement? How much are you willing to gamble for long-term security? The same sets of suggested questions apply to other professions.

The linking of professional and personal goals is part of module 1—not just your current goals but planning your life.

Social goals: The articulation of aims and goals could include not only children and significant others and friendships but parents and how much time will you need to fulfill these goals.

Ethical goals: Other goals involve the creation of personal meaning. They may be spiritual goals, existential needs, humanistic needs, and a sense of purpose.

The articulation of personal and business goals is a holistic process. Consider whether and how you can coordinate social, personal, and ethical goals. The process should help you become more aware of all these goals and how your desired professional life may change the relative value that you place on each of these goals.

Module 2: Articulation of Difficulties, Frustrations, Obstacles, and Conflicts

Inevitably you will encounter frustrations and setbacks in meeting those larger goals. Whether you are an entrepreneur, investor, or film producer, creating a business plan that will be successful means being able to think both in terms of potential problems and goals. How quickly do you recognize problems? Are you even open to the possibility that what you envisioned might not work out? To what extent can you perceive frustrations? A plan should be realistic in anticipating impediments and identifying strategies for dealing with them. Make sure that you have an objective understanding of some of the problems that might arise in your business or profession that are not related to yourself. How would you deal with these external problems? What would you need to do psychologically to deal with them, and how would they affect your ability to deal with the rest of your life?

Concrete questions to ask include the following: What objective potential problems could affect your business? How will your plan enable you to deal with those contingencies? What other contingencies can occur to disrupt the plan? Think through potential problems. Develop several scenarios of contingencies that are built into the business plan.

Also ask: What are your fears? What other internal impediments do you see that might block you from achieving your professional and personal goals?

How will you deal with failure? Can you even imagine you could fail? Can you anticipate what would happen if your plan does not work? What alternative plans can you develop if the plan fails?

Modules 1 and 2: Articulation of the Field

Link modules 1 and 2 in terms of (a) goals and (b) what may hold you back in terms of achieving them. At the same time, think how the goals (module 1) and potential threats (module 2) are related. They may affect different goals differently. While thinking through these questions, spend one session on each of the four areas: how you would deal with professional impediments, personal impediments, social obstacles, and ethical obstacles.

One area to link involves the balance of work issues with personal issues. How will you connect your professional goals to your other goals? How will your professional life fit with your personal goals? Certain vocational failures can interfere with your personal life.

Remember to link the various personal goals while you focus on the impediments to each. This linkage is part of the active coping framework. Passive coping is to cut off your personal life. For example, to deny that suddenly becoming an entrepreneur or professional photographer will affect your spouse or children is to be coping passively. Active coping is to think about your business life and connect it to your overall life goals. You need a personal plan, a life plan. This is where developmental differences come into play. If you're fifty years old, your ambitions might be very different than if you're in your thirties. If you're in your thirties, you might want to build an organization. If you're in your fifties, you might want a last chance to do your own thing, pursue a passion you have withheld in order to provide for your family.

Spend time understanding your personal motivations as well as fears, risks, and potential impediments. Try to articulate the personal dimensions and link them to the professional dimension.

Then link the professional back to the personal dimensions and try to understand how and why they both relate to your desired undertaking.

The holistic linking of these parts is where trying to self-assess without help is tough. But even if you're not working with someone to give you feedback, give it a try. What are your personal goals? What are the sources of problems? How do you see your Gestalt, the pattern of your behavior as a whole, as distinct from the parts that make up this pattern?

In summary, the first part of module 2 is to identify the problems. Can you see them? The next is to link modules 1 and 2. Can you see all the complexity? Try to see and tolerate the complexity in order to ensure that it does not become so overwhelming that you run away from it. This is the linkage of modules 1 and 2. Remember that while you are linking these various areas, what you are trying to develop is catalytic coping.

Module 3: Catalytic Coping

Catalytic coping is the adaptive side of coping. It is seeing the reality of the situation and playing the game the way you need to play it. It is the capacity to respond flexibly and adaptively as the situation presents itself. Resourcefulness, creativity, persistence, and stamina—assess yourself: where will you not deal as adaptively and effectively as you should, and how can you develop yourself to overcome or circumvent that aspect of your coping style? First look at past patterns, then identify possible negative coping strategies, and while you are doing that make sure you don't engage in those at crucial points as you are pursuing your professional goals.

Once you have planned, questions you might ask regarding the personal and business sides of the plan include the following: How will you actually deal with the issues as they arise? Do you truly have the psychological strength to carry out the plan? How will you continue to develop it? Do you have the emotional capacity to deal with contingencies that arise without giving up? How will you develop that capacity to adapt to contingencies?

Questions you might ask in dealing with the social realm include the following: How do you connect with others in carrying out the business plan? How will you deal with investors, directors, employees, customers, and suppliers? What is your strategy for relating to others? Are you authoritarian? Can you delegate? What are your social skills dealing with customers? How will you deal with multiple demands on your family and friends? In the pursuit of your professional aims, what are you going to do in terms of a spouse, children, a significant other, friends, or aging parents? What will be your strategies for dealing with these aspects of your life?

Suggested questions you might ask yourself in at least gaining an awareness of psychological autonomy, which contributes to catalytic coping, include the following: Can you empathize with others without dominating or overidealizing them and losing yourself? Can you maintain sufficient independence of mind to come up with what you think is fair—rather than overvalue, minimize, or devalue others? Can you recognize others' needs, consider others' feelings, and maintain your independent mind? Can you articulate a vision that others can believe in? Can you communicate a goal so that everyone who needs to buy into it actually does?

Do you have a way to recognize when you're likely to make a suboptimal decision? Can you tell when you're comfortable moving ahead because your perception of the issue from a business and psychological perspective is adequate? Can you recognize when your psyche gets in the way of seeing things with 20-20 vision and coming up with an appropriate response? When that happens, do you have the guts and self-control to postpone a decision so you can talk it through with someone or gather more information? Do you have the good judgment to see where a mentor is necessary, or when you need to consult with someone, and with whom? Can you discern that if you are feeling burned out, stressed, anxious, or angry, you would do well to take time out and talk to someone? Have a list of three people with whom you would talk. Have the discipline to take the time out and give your mind time to relax.

You may have blind spots. Try describing your self-assessment to someone you know and trust, who may be able to see your defensive tactics as well as your active coping tendencies and help you to see them, too. It may be useful to make a checklist of issues and situations, ones in which your immediate decisions may not be the best ones although they initially may make you feel good. At those times you may not be able to make your best decisions; your ability to perceive clearly is less than adequate.

At this point, it may be extremely important to ask yourself how you have coped with problems in the past. Do you see evidence of running away? Does your work history show a change in jobs every three years? If so, is that because you repeatedly reached a limit of your coping and hence you left? Identify past coping or defensive patterns throughout your whole life, both professional and personal, and how you have dealt with problems. Have you balanced multiple demands in the past? If not, be careful not to repeat patterns that got you into trouble in the past.

If you left corporate America to start a new venture, for example, consider why you left. Did you leave in anger? Do you have problems with authority figures and want to be independent? Independence can be wonderful, but even entrepreneurs need to deal with people (customers, investors, employees, etc.) who may arouse that same hostility. In any profession, you have to interact with forces bigger than you. Don't run away from those you view as authority figures; don't run away from forces bigger than you. Figure out what sets off maladaptive coping tendencies. Also, look for signs of magical thinking. By that, I mean imagining that everything will turn out great when things get difficult.

Module 4: Integrity

Maintaining self-esteem under stress while behaving with integrity is another area to consider. If you want to have self-esteem and self-confidence, then you must behave in a way that supports your stated and unstated values. The relationship between self-esteem and integrity was integral to the discussion in chapter 5. Throughout your self-assessment, ask yourself how you maintain self-esteem under stress. This module suffuses modules 1, 2, and 3. It allows you to plan and to cope adaptively. Knowing what the issues will be, do you have the confidence to go ahead, and will you be happy doing it?

As you examine yourself, you may ask yourself if you can maintain self-esteem without resorting to denial, avoidance, and similar passive reactions to deal with threats. Can you deal with the losses, threats, and fears of pursuing your professional goals without their breaking down your psychological system? Can you handle stress, failure, and loss and recoup? How do you handle challenges? How do you handle threats to your self-esteem? Can you imagine a scenario where the threat to self-esteem would be so great that you might use means other than active coping to deal with the situation (say, suicide, homicide, embezzlement)? Some individuals under stress behave in ways that leave them feeling ashamed. At many points, one is tempted to cheat, to lie, or to bend the law, with or without rationalizing such actions.

Stress can result in psychological symptoms. Do you know the signs of stress and anxiety? Also, look at the major problems others in your profession have—failure of the business, resisting temptations (taking short cuts, fraud, embezzlement rather than active coping), or other mental health issues (depression, burn out, somatization).

Module 4 is where you draw your psychological and social resources together. Is your psyche such that you are able to use your resources appropriately? The business plan and the personal plan converge, and *you* own the plan.

Module 4 brings up the issue of self. The self runs throughout this module because it influences all of your motives. The idea of the self is that it is part of the psyche that has the capacity to respond actively and autonomously in coping with novel and stressful situations.

Given your professional, personal, and interpersonal goals and the efforts it will take to resolve them, you have to decide whether you will have enough energy left after making these efforts to maintain self-esteem. Do you think you'll be happy doing it? Given what it will take, is this for you? Will you be happy with the sacrifices? Consider the investment of time and the tradeoffs you will have to make. Do you think you will be left with feeling confident and satisfied?

Ask yourself the following questions:

1. Do you have the confidence to carry out this plan? As a self, can you handle it? Do you feel you have enough confidence and trust in yourself to carry it through?

2. Are you going to be happy doing it? When you look at all the problems and what you have to do in order to contend with them, the time you have to invest, and the sacrifices you'll have to make in your life, are you going to feel good about these sacrifices? Is this really what you want to do?

Modules 1 and 2 outlined the conscious goals and the impediments to achieving these goals of which you may or may not be aware. Module 3 asked you, while you are doing your planning, to look for some of the unconscious and semiconscious forces in you that make it easier or harder to deal with these goals and impediments. Module 4 asked you to look at your goals and sacrifices in light of your innermost ideals and beliefs.

First, can you develop a sound plan (combining your professional and personal plan)? Are you able to see reality, the good parts and the bad, and plan for how to deal with possible impediments, frustrations, threats, and conflicts?

Second, do you have the psychological strength to deal with obstacles that might come up to challenge the actual execution of the professional plan? If the plan doesn't work out, do you have the flexibility to alter your approach to develop new strategies to achieve your aims and goals? Do you have the creativity and resourcefulness to survive changes (social, legal, technological, economic)?

You have to be flexible to cope with these changes while considering the implications of what you do to cope with the changes. It's an attempt to understand *what this professional goal means to you as a human being*.

If, at the end of the self-assessment, you feel that your coping style is passive for any reason, do not give up. Recall the multi-level typology described in chapter 5. The four columns refer to possible combinations of an individual's coping style at the overt, easily observable (by self and others and therefore conscious), semiconscious, and unconscious levels. Particularly, if you decide you are an LHH type—weak on the surface but stronger deep down, the surface passivity may be the result of socialization and more amenable to change than the passive coping at the unconscious level. LHH types may have underlying reservoirs of activity that have been suppressed and do not appear in their overt behavior. You may not be aware of these deeper resources of power. But you can draw on them, if you have them, to develop an active coping style through and through—the HHH type.

Outcomes and Benefits

The self-assessment program should build and strengthen your ability to develop the emotional capacity and psychological strength to carry out your professional plan without sacrificing your personal and social goals or abandoning your moral principles. There's a kind of psychological synchronicity that has to track the competitive environment of the venture. This program should yield enhanced understanding of yourself and operationally useful insights and enhanced capacity to learn from setbacks and defeats.

Outcomes and benefits of such an assessment include gaining a greater understanding of how your psyche may get in the way of seeing opportunities and addressing them in an adaptive way, enhanced self-awareness and self-esteem, and enhanced catalytic coping. In twenty weeks, you should have an advanced understanding of yourself. Most of us have blind spots. Assuming you have enough active coping to become aware of them, you should also begin to understand how you maintain self-esteem as well as understand how stress can manifest itself (for example, depression, anxiety, physical illness).

Even a successful self-assessment is only a beginning. If you follow this program, in twenty weeks, your psyche should at least be on its way to becoming your ally instead of your adversary in dealing with professional problems as you go forward. When you complete this program, you should understand yourself and your issues better and be in a better position to deal with them realistically. You may also gain operationally useful insights into the ventures in which you are engaged or which you plan to undertake.

At the very least, this twenty-week self-assessment should make you ready for professional assistance to turn your new insights and understanding into appropriate patterns of behavior.

12

Developing Active Coping:
A Success Story

ONE EXECUTIVE WHOM I have known since 1998 makes a case for active coping as a developmental process.[1] This executive grew up in a blue-collar small town, the only child of a first-generation immigrant family. His parents, aunts, and uncles did not speak English. Sixty-three years after his birth, he is approaching the pinnacle of his career, having served as CFO of two Fortune 500 Companies, as CFO and partner at an international private equity firm, and on multiple boards.

What allowed him to allow that success to occur—beyond the fact that he is bright, charismatic, and forceful? What enabled him to deploy his psychological resources to become the highly sought after board member and investor that he currently is?

He told this story to me, and it aptly illustrates each of the elements of active coping described in this book:

> One of the things I have had to fight my whole life is a sense of not being good enough. Growing up in a small town in basically a redneck community where I was of immigrant parents where

basically everybody's last name was one syllable and mine was three, I got this negative reinforcement. The environment was discriminatory, and I was always being told, "You're not good enough because of where you came from and what your people do." My guidance counselor told me that "Your type of people ought to go into learning a trade" and that I ought to go to trade school and become an auto mechanic when I graduated thirteenth out of something like 585 kids.

This high school student overcame this bias, as indicated by the following paragraph:

It was always the economic part that motivated me. I wanted to be with the kids who had the money and I was excluded from activities because my parents didn't belong to the country club. But those were the cool kids, and I wanted to show them that "I can be one of you." So a big motivator for me was to show them that I could become wealthy and overcome all of the obstacles put in my way. But I had to overcome in myself being told, "You're not good enough, you don't fit, you didn't go to the right school" and that was a limiter of what I was going to be.

Overcoming the ethnic bias of his original community is an example of catalytic coping kicking into play.

As a boy, this executive wanted to become a Catholic priest. But as an adolescent, he tried to shut off his sensitive, caring, empathic, spiritual side:

I made a vow to myself when I was fifteen years old. I used to be sensitive, afraid of my own shadow, always wanted to please everybody until I finally got fed up and made up my mind that nobody was ever going to hurt me again. I made a vow to myself that I was going to be the toughest person I could be in every dimension—physical, mental, emotional, and walled myself off so I wouldn't be hurt.

Next he describes integrity and integrative capacity:

> Eventually I had to integrate the two sides of myself: the soft side that wanted to become a priest but was bullied and the side that wanted to dominate every situation so as never to be bullied again because inside myself I was still this kid who was pretty sensitive and tender hearted. The public me wasn't the real me. A lot of that came out in marriage counseling, which led me to become more authentic.

This set of statements relate to the linkage of modules 1 and 2 introduced in the previous chapter. And, consistent with the strong advice to have someone whom you know and trust to help you to change, he indicates the importance of having someone one trusts as a mentor or other counselor in helping one change:

> Obviously now because I've had some success, I've achieved goals in life I never dreamed of achieving, I know it's no longer a problem and I know the myth now has been destroyed but wanting to please this person, wanting everyone to love you was a hard battle to fight every day. What I've found is eventually you've got to get to the point where you're comfortable with yourself even though you may have anxiety that it's not going to turn out the way you'd like it to turn out, if there's nothing better that you can think you can do even if it seems to antagonize or alienate certain people, you are still willing to press forward with it.

In the foregoing paragraph, he describes both psychological autonomy and how it helps him pursue the path he deems optimal: in other words, catalytic coping. It relates to module 3. In the following paragraph he touches on integrity and how psychological autonomy supports an authentic self:

> Even if people don't like it, you still press forward with it . . .
> even if they are upset about it, they can't criticize me for doing
> the wrong thing in terms of an ethical or moral basis.

Next he talks again about the active coping as an ongoing process
over the course of one's life:

> I didn't unfortunately always have that knowledge. I developed
> it later in life. Learning involves feedback. The career counseling
> aspects of having a mentor are very important; otherwise, with
> whom do you consult? Working with you, I have developed
> more appreciation for how the factors involved in active coping
> come together, but it is a very complex concept and something
> you don't learn about when you are going through school.

Regarding leadership, psychological autonomy and integrity,
and summoning the courage to press forward with what he thinks
is the right thing to do, this executive also stated the following,
stressing more clearly the role of integrity as the glue that keeps
his psychological system together:

> I continue to battle within myself uncertainty, anxiety, motiva-
> tion, sometime sheer fatigue, "Phew, I've been fighting this for
> months and I would just like it to go away." But at the end of
> the day, where I find peace generally is when I realize that things
> aren't going to turn out the way I that think they should turn
> out, I can worry less about the decisions that I'm making and
> just be comfortable that I am operating within the boundaries
> I have set for myself in terms of proper behavior. Some degree of
> psychological comfort is always present; you are always going
> to weigh these tensions that you have on yourself, the tensions
> that arise from personal acceptance, to risk, to overcoming
> anxiety, to overcoming fear, but in a leadership position, if you

can't have that ability to tolerate psychological discomfort, by definition you can't lead.

In other words, psychological autonomy and integrity are part of his style of being. And he continued his reflections on leadership and active coping:

> When I think of these four elements of active coping, it's not just the leader who has to have these qualities; they all have to fit together around the leadership of the company. Even in interviewing for board members, I have to be able to spot board members who know how to contribute without being invasive, who understand the difference between setting policy and setting tactics.

Active coping characterizes not only individuals but also teams, implied in the following statements by him:

> The first thing is there has to be self-awareness because you need a baseline of where I am now. The difficulty is that we all have a different self-image or perception of ourselves from how others perceive us and we are completely oblivious to how we are coming across versus how we *think* we are coming across. When you get that wake up call, it's like getting hit between the eyes with an iron rod: "You have got to be kidding! I actually thought I was this type of person and everyone is telling me, no, you're really a jerk."

He continued to talk about developing active coping, first about developing it through formal objective feedback to one executive and active coping as it applies to every member of the management team:

> That's where an overall assessment, a 360-degree assessment, where an objective professional gathers information about how

you are perceived by those with whom you work, is very beneficial. It's like getting mumps at a later age. The older you are before you get it, all of a sudden for somebody to tell you, "You don't do everything perfectly; the world at large thinks you're a schmoe" is pretty tough to take. But you do have to get a starting point, an assessment based on the tools used to make that assessment, then a measurement process to see where you are today, and where you are two years from now, and four years from now. I can see companies actually helping develop people in a more rational way by taking that approach, especially the management talent of the company, as opposed to sending them to a seminar to learn a particular technique.

Then actually bringing it down into the elements of active coping where development has to occur, anywhere from psychological autonomy to catalytic coping. A lot of times they are related: You are a pleaser or you are a martyr or you have codependent qualities you need to become aware of. Then can you overcome them? How deep seated are they? How tightly do you have Linus's security blanket in your grasp? If you don't know where you are today, you don't know where to begin to develop.

Once again, he emphasizes the importance of active coping as openness to integrating information and using that information to grow. Again, speaking of the feedback and others in changing oneself, he stated,

It's hard to change if you're not in a trusting relationship. Surrounding yourself with a more intimate group or a counselor willing to confront you with your behavior, with whom you feel safe to expose the private person hiding behind the public person, allows you begin to see the real you versus how you really act.

These statements demonstrate each element of active coping as a style of functioning, an overall positive orientation to life that supports ongoing growth and adaptation. They also illustrate each of the elements of the active coping style discussed in this book.

13

Conclusion

LOOKS GOOD ON PAPER? presents one model to understand personality as a whole, a model that takes into account unconscious forces and developmental history. I argue that it is possible to predict, at least much of the time, how an executive is likely to cope with unexpected complexities and changes. The book presents a method, corresponding to the model, for assessing personality structure and dynamics.

Central to my approach is an attempt to examine what I have called a person's active coping style, though this alone does not necessarily predict leadership potential successfully. Intelligence, motivation, and the context—the culture of the organization and the broader culture within which that organization is embedded—are also very important. But they are not the whole story. The approach I illustrate in this book tries to examine and understand the whole person, not just what's inside, and not just what looks good on paper.

Part I focuses on how this method can add significant information in assessing executives who have already met the normal criteria for being considered for senior leadership roles, principally based on their experience and the reports of people with whom they have worked. It describes the four interrelated elements of the active coping style that are crucial to predicting leadership: integrity, psychological autonomy, integrative capacity, and catalytic coping. To illustrate and explain these elements of active coping and their interrelations, I have drawn principally on examples of executives I have assessed and to some extent on examples of well-known leaders from history.

Part II suggests that it is possible, up to a point, to conduct and profit from a self-assessment, particularly if one has the help of a mentor, who could be a trusted friend, a relative, or even a therapist. Not everyone will benefit fully, or at all, from a self-assessment—or from a professional in-depth assessment. Chapter 11 discusses the issues this raises both generally and with examples of how individuals changed or failed to change long after their formative years, analyzing them by reference to particular elements of active coping. The following chapter presents a short how-to guide for a twenty-week self-assessment. Part II concludes with the story of a man who came from humble origins and rose to great success. The lesson of his story is a lesson in the vitality and resiliency of the self as it grows and continues to grow and learn from experience.

In closing, some caveats. Most of my direct experience has been with white American men being considered for leadership positions in American businesses. Chapter 10 tries to examine the implications for women aspiring to leadership roles. I point out, for example, that for men to be effective leaders, it appears that they are free to be either agentic (aggressive, exhibitionistic, domineering, and the like) or communal (nurturing, playful, and open to aesthetic experiences), at least in appropriate situations. For a woman to be an effective leader she too must be able to act in an agentic fashion when necessary, but she is much better off if she is not perceived as having an agentic style. This may be changing as more women move into the higher ranks of American corporations and American political life and as a younger generation comes of age.

Still, how the assessment system described in this book would work on assessing women for leadership positions is an open question. More generally, as I have mentioned, with a few exceptions I have not assessed business leaders abroad, including Americans who are going to work abroad. To be successful, an aspiring CEO's personality and talents must jive with the culture of the organization he is to lead and the business climate in which it is or will be operating. What defeated George Fisher (who was so successful at Motorola) at Kodak was ultimately Kodak's culture. Cultural values, educational systems, business practices, and gender perceptions and relations are different in Europe and from country to country within Europe. Even table manners (the "lack" of which does not help, to say the least) are different in a few but very noticeable ways between the United States and Europe.

With the development of an international business world with a global market and international business corporations large and small, I hope that this book will stimulate new research in how widely my methods apply and how they should be adjusted where they apply at all. But I hope even more that the analysis in this book, the descriptions of the four elements of the active coping style, the illustrative life stories, and the self-assessment suggestions in part II will resonate with readers, whether they are executives, artists, or young adults in the process of forming an identity, encourage them to probe more deeply into their own psyches, and inspire greater insight into their own and others' actions.

Technical Companion to Chapter 3

Origins and Conceptual Clarification of Coping Style

In the early days of psychoanalytic theory, Freud took the tragic and rather simplistic view that you either repress your drives to be civilized or you do not and cannot function in society. This theory produces a rather unrealistic picture of human society: on one side Civilization, on the other its Discontents.

The ego psychologists started from Freud's theory but modified and extended it. They believed that not all human behavior was necessarily a product of conflict and posited a zone of functioning that in healthy individuals is free of conflict and relatively independent of internal desires and superego compulsions (such as a constant striving to be "perfect"). This zone of conflict-free functioning develops as a process of internalizing cultural norms and is created by an ego that is active and therefore relatively independent of internal drives and external pressures. Active coping allows you to take in information from both your internal desires and external responsibilities and to consider how *you* want to respond without capitulating to either source of pressure.

The *Oxford Dictionary*'s first definition of "cope," as in "to cope with," is "to deal effectively or contend successfully with a person or task." The second definition is to "manage successfully; deal with a situation or problem." As synonyms, it offers terms such as "to withstand," "to handle," "to get by," "to make do," "to survive," "to subsist," "to muddle through," or "to scrape by." These definitions reverberate negatively with many people, but I use the term active coping in a positive sense, and I wish to use this section to clarify conceptually the origins and history of the construct of coping style and the terms "active coping" and "passive coping."

Since Freud, "activity" and "passivity" have been crucial factors qualifying the ego in depth-psychological theories of personality analysis. In psychology, the concept of coping emerged in the context of clinical work and research on stress-induced psychopathology, prevention, and treatment. The term "coping" for a psychological construct came into wider use after it appeared in the 1958 edition of the *Comprehensive Dictionary of Psychological and Psychoanalytical Terms*. There it was defined as "action that enables one to adjust to the environmental circumstances."[1] This definition construes coping as a mechanism of adjustment, implicitly goal oriented but essentially a reaction to external stimuli. It ignores the "valence"[2] of circumstances, whether positive (challenging or potentially satisfying) or negative (threatening the immediate satisfaction of basic needs and/or the potential for further development). It views coping as a reaction to a specific situation. This orientation fit the spirit of logical positivist behaviorism so prominent in psychology in the United States during the early and mid-1950s. In experimental work, "coping" appears in research carried out mostly on rats and college freshmen. This viewpoint did not illuminate the complexities of human coping behavior, even under relatively simple conditions.

The most important roots of the concept of *coping style* reach back through the psychosocial movement of positive mental health[3] and midcentury psychoanalytically oriented ego psychology to Freud's definition of the ego, which reads:

> [The ego] has the task of self-preservation. As regards external events, it performs that task by becoming aware of stimuli, by storing up experiences about them (in the memory), by avoiding excessively strong stimuli (through flight), by dealing with moderate stimuli (through adaptation) and finally by learning to bring about expedient changes in the external world to its own advantage (through activity). As regards internal events, in relation to the id, it performs that task by gaining control over the demands of the instincts, by deciding whether they are to be allowed satisfaction, by postponing that satisfaction to times and circumstances favorable in the external world or by suppressing their excitations entirely.[4]

This definition depicts the ego as a complex system of behaviors. These behaviors integrate experience in a way that permits the reality-oriented use of past development in the process of coping with new situations. A sense of time and a changing reality are implied, both of which are necessary for the delay of gratification. Control over instinctual demands and voluntary movement and learning to modify the conditions of existence are conditions for adequate ego functioning. Freud portrays the ego as an active system and *not* passive in the sense of mainly reacting to internal or external pressures. Rather, he describes it as a central integrating and steering mechanism capable of addressing issues that may arise at different stages of development or in any one act or experience.

After World War II, this definition of the ego became an essential element in the development of the branch of psychoanalytic thinkings known as ego psychology, most notably theorized by Heinz Hartmann,[5] David Rapaport, Erik Erikson, and others. Hartmann most clearly advanced the idea of ego autonomy. He posited that the ego is not entirely a derivative of drives. Ultimately, this led to a revision of the classical psychoanalytic position on the nature of developmental processes, including their extension over a lifetime. One of the early lifespan developmental psychologists was Erik Erikson. In the 1960s, he assigned to the ego "the domain of inner agency safeguarding our coherent existence by screening and synthesizing in any series of movements all the impressions, emotions, memories, and impulses which try to enter our thought and demand our action and which would tear us apart, if unsorted and unmanaged."[6] Erikson condensed this statement to say that the ego's overall task is to turn passive into active. The meaning of active and passive in this context is similar to that of Rapaport, who viewed passivity as a state of "uncontrolled drive demand both in its helplessness . . . and in its effortless passive gratification," whereas activity is "a state of ego control both in its defensive . . . and executive aspect."[7]

Rapaport also stressed the relativity of the activity-passivity polarity, noting that most of our actions and experiences are actually a result of some combination of both. That is, not all defensive operations are passive under all conditions, nor is all action always activity. Activity and passivity refer only partly to overt observable behavior. Mostly, they refer to unconscious parameters of ego functioning. The active-passive factor also reflects the extent to which the ego has achieved autonomy from the drives in terms of independence of energy supply. In other words, it marks developmental progression or regression as well.

Another group of authors also started to work on this topic in the late 1950s and early 1960s. They endeavored to clarify the distinction between coping behavior and defense mechanisms, both of which they treated as ego functions.[8] Among the first of these authors to use the concept of coping in empirical research on personality development was Lois Murphy. She differentiated among coping devices, defensive behavior, and automatic reactions and tended to view any effortful attempt at "mastery" as coping. Beginning in the late 1950s, David Gutmann also treated coping in terms of mastery.[9] He viewed mastery as mostly internal, a technique bridging unconscious processes and demands from the sociocultural environment. In his theory, development throughout life proceeds from what he called an active mastery stance, to passive mastery, to magical mastery.

During the 1950s, interest in the relationships among personality, perception, and thought led yet another group of authors to experimental work on cognitive styles and their role in adaptation, mental health, and psychopathology. By seeking to identify principles of psychological organization that could explain dimensions of the transaction between the person and the environment, their work was a precursor for viewing coping behavior as a style of functioning.

Beginning in the 1980s, in contrast to the above noted approaches, Richard Lazarus and his coauthors developed a cognitive-behavioral approach to the concept of coping. In it, they emphasize the observable and consciously controlled aspects of the coping process in contrast to psychoanalytic perspectives.[10] Such cognitive-behavioral approaches are useful for describing "ways of coping" understood as "person in encounter." But they refer neither to the parameters of the person nor to those of the encounter. As such, they cannot be used to predict longer and more psychologically meaningful periods of human development. Of course, situational factors affect and interact with subjective perception, but longitudinal studies of adult development and aging show that stability rather than change is the norm for personality parameters such as coping style.[11]

Joel Shanan, cited in appendix B, conceptualized coping style as a manifestation of ego functioning. In his model, like those of Gutmann and Murphy, coping behavior does not refer primarily to overt activity but mostly to internal emotive-cognitive processes. Overt behavior is part of a process initiated by an interpretation of what is going on in one's internal and external environment.

Appendix A

The theory of active coping as I have used in my assessments and research builds on the thinking of Shanan and the ego psychologists noted previously in this section. For example, Rapaport's works on ego autonomy heavily influenced the element of active coping that I have defined and called "psychological autonomy."

Technical Companion to Chapter 4

Assessment Methods and Measures

In psychological assessment, tests can be highly structured, semi-structured, or unstructured. This dimension refers to the degree to which a test does or does not have a high degree of specificity in the tasks involved. Structured tests tend to be close to the concept of questions with right and wrong answers. The more the test permits the individual to use his or her own ideas and imagination in responding to the task, the less structured the situation is. For the most structured tests, the tasks are specific, with little opportunity for the respondent to make an individual interpretation of the task. For unstructured tests, the tasks are vague and unfamiliar, and they require that the respondent contribute much to the interpretation of the task itself. The tests within the battery of tests that I use represent these three levels of structure.

Examples of structured tests include personality inventories (*true* means this statement describes me; *false*, this statement does not describe me) or the Graduate Management Aptitude Test. Tasks are so highly defined that the respondent is fully aware of what is expected of him or her—to find the standard answer rather than

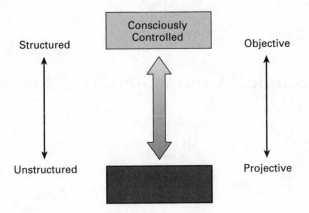

APP.B.I Psychological Assessment Methods

the one reflecting personal choice. Because the task requires that the individual respond with a prescribed answer, her responses provide little information about her uniqueness as a person.

Indeed, on structured tasks, the more unique the respondent's answers, the stronger the inference that an internal psychological process has become so powerful that it has pervaded the situation from which the respondent should be able to exclude it. In such situations, straightforward, objective questions do not bring forth straightforward, objective answers. Instead, answers are so colored by the invading personalized material that they spoil the appropriateness of the response and reflect a diminished capacity for coping with everyday situations.

In contrast, with unstructured tests, the respondent has minimal information regarding the demands of the task. That means that the respondent must turn to his or her own personal resources to formulate what the task involves and how to cope with it.

Reviewing a person's responses to structured, semistructured, and unstructured tests makes possible comparative inferences on all three levels of personality, to assess whether the person has the capacity to cope effectively with all three types of demands. If the respondent is not successful on all three, then I note whether there is difficulty only in the more personal, unstructured situation, whether the difficulty is more pervasive and includes difficulty at the semistructured level, or whether the difficulties permeate all aspects of functioning.

By mapping this continuum of structured to semistructured to unstructured situations onto life situations, one can understand the degree to which an individual is dependent on external guidance and direction for effective coping. One definition of the effective and emotionally healthy person (and the one that I use) is based on the concept of the capacity to cope with most of life's situations, ranging from those that permit little initiative to those that require a great deal of initiative. A battery of tests, of the type just described, provides a basis for judging the individual's ability to match that definition. From this description, one might expect that more effective coping on unstructured psychological tests would differentiate effective from ineffective leaders and that active coping across the three levels assessed would characterize the most effective leaders.

Closely related to the structured-unstructured continuum in psychological assessment is the objective-projective dimension. Objective assessment techniques represent clear, unambiguous stimuli that permit a high degree of conscious control over what is revealed about the self. Consequently, such techniques assess more peripheral (that is, easily observable) aspects of personality functioning. Individuals who are successful by normative standards find it easy to fall back on the structure of the test to produce what they understand to be the desired image. In particular, most candidates for senior leadership positions are already quite good at behaving appropriately and are skilled at monitoring their responses. Consequently, objective techniques are poor predictors of leadership among managers contending for senior leadership roles.

Projective techniques, in contrast to objective assessment techniques, present the respondent with relatively vague and ambiguous stimuli, to which the respondent must interpret. The interpretation involves projection of the respondent's psyche, eliciting underlying personality characteristics. Like unstructured tests, the stimuli provide little structure to guide the response. They thereby reveal aspects of psychological functioning related to underlying structural dimensions that are inaccessible with objective tests. Projective techniques are especially well suited to assess active coping, because meeting the demand of partial ambiguity in the test-taking situation requires the mobilization of energy and orientation of attention inherent in active coping.

Projective Techniques

Self-report methods have their place in the assessment and hiring process. I conduct interviews, read résumés, and use my own questionnaires. These methods are useful and test for different qualities.[1] I also use projective techniques. Projective techniques are tests that present vague, ambiguous stimuli—an ambiguous picture, a sentence fragment—and require the test taker to respond to each stimulus. The ambiguity of the stimulus requires them to pull spontaneously an unscripted response from within themselves.

A sentence completion test is one example of a semiprojective technique. It is a test I administer on the spot to elicit a series of responses, each item of which provides a partial structure that must be completed spontaneously by the candidate.

An active coping response to that stem might be, "When he failed in his work . . . he resolved to try again but prepared for the outcome." Or, "When she failed in her work . . . she became introspective and attempted to learn from her failure." These two items demonstrate active, autonomous efforts to deal with the source of stress; the response is either cognitive or else it describes an actual series of actions set in motion by the failure.

A passive coping response might be, "When he felt the chances were lost . . . he started to cry." Or, "When she felt that others kept distant . . . she increasingly kept to herself." These responses do not deal actively or autonomously with the source of stress, cognitively or behaviorally. Another example of a passive coping response is, "Failure made him . . . bitter." An active coping response would be, "Failure made him . . . learn from his failure to become stronger," indicating that the test subject integrated the failure and learned from it.

What if someone just refuses to answer? If the test taker does not complete a sentence stem, then he has refused to cope with the task. He has demonstrated a breakdown in coping, at least in response to that stem.

The most powerful projective technique that I use to assess leaders is a projective storytelling technique. It uses a set of pictures, to each of which the candidate must tell a story evoked by the picture. The pictures are designed to elicit paradigmatic themes in human development. Those I have selected to use are most relevant to leadership situations.

The projective storytelling technique enables a clinical psychologist to pull together various aspects collected via the other assessment techniques with motives, coping, interpersonal relatedness, degree of optimism, and outcomes.

Interpreting the stories involves many observations, too numerous to cite here. But the process of interpretation depends on two tentative assumptions, which may subsequently change. One is that the attributes of the characters in the stories represent tendencies in the subject's personality and represent potentially latent or active forces. The other is that forces in the story represent forces in the subject's environment, as he experienced, experiences, or expects to experience it, which may be interpreted as impressions he is likely to project onto his perceptions of existing and possible future situations.

Although many more interpretive steps are taken, clinical psychologists are taught to treat each conclusion when analyzing projective storytelling technique stories as working hypotheses—not proven facts—to be verified, revised, or refuted by other material gleaned from the assessment. The structure and content of a set of stories represent a covert level of personality, not the overt, public persona. As such, the projective storytelling technique is one of the few methods available for uncovering covert tendencies. Different tests of reliability (test-retest and interrater reliability, internal consistency) of the projective storytelling technique are found in publications using the test for research into personality development.[2]

Interviews with the clients requesting the assessment that require the clients to define rigorously the characteristics a successful candidate would need to possess in conjunction with the key elements of the operating environment, a self-report measure of personality, a life history interview, the sentence completion technique, and the projective storytelling technique all make up the battery of tests I administer that yields responses at three levels of functioning, corresponding to the method of data collection: self-report, semiprojective, and projective tests—the conscious, semiconscious, and unconscious.

A Structural Model of Personality

Mine is not the only structural model of personality in existence. It is essentially an extension of the later Freud's structural model of the personality, modified by Jung and Freud's successors in ego psychology (most importantly, Hartmann and Rappaport) and, most recently, self-psychology (Kohut).

The *id* is a set of functions, not a physical place. It comprises two constant psychological forces, a constructive force and a destructive force. These forces constitute the basic energy sources for the personality. The constructive force is the source of feelings of love, creativity, and psychological growth. The destructive force gives rise to feelings of anger and hostility. The twin forces are variously called love and hate, sex and aggression. Human beings have to fuse them so that the constructive force can temper, guide, and control the destructive force and so that the energy from both sources may be channeled to promote the person's growth and survival.

The id includes the needs that derive from the two forces. As human beings, we have biological needs, self-esteem needs, social needs, and aesthetic needs. For example, we need to eat and be safe; we need to feel worthy and capable of directing our lives; we need to belong; we need to feel connected and that our lives have meaning. Some individuals have competitive needs such as needs to dominate, control, possess wealth, or exercise power. Some also have needs to develop intellectually, athletically, or artistically. At the most basic level, we all need pleasure.

In addition to internal needs, the id stores memories and experiences that a person can no longer recall but which might be expressed if they were not controlled. Often, a person forgets or represses these memories. Repression is the process of pushing experiences that may be too painful to recall into the unconscious. The id can conflict with superego demands and constraints because it operates according to the pleasure principle: "I want what I want when I want it."

The *superego* helps us balance or fuse constructive and destructive forces in our selves and finds ways to express them in socially acceptable ways. Culture specifies how love and aggression are expressed, and members socialized within a culture internalize the values and ideals that the culture promotes. The particular controls vary from culture to culture, even from one social class to another. They are transmitted to children through parents and other authority figures. (A parental relationship need not be with one's parents. There may be other powerfully influential individuals in our lives who play a parental role, particularly as role models.)

Early in a child's development, parents control and direct the child. Parents permit some forms of behavior but prohibit others. As children grow older, they incorporate the values their parents have taught them. Children who feel an affectionate bond with their parents and want to be like them will incorporate these rules and values most effectively. As children become more self-governing, Freud would say they are acquiring a superego. In Freud's last revision to his model, the superego had two components: the conscience and the ego ideal. The function of the conscience is to perceive any proscribed thought, feeling, or behavior and then produce guilt should those thoughts be expressed. Conscience is like a built-in governor, the internalized civilizing agent, a voice that expresses itself in anxieties we experience around behaviors we have learned not to express. The ego ideal represents images to which we aspire, consciously and unconsciously, and against which we measure ourselves. It is based on identification with parents and other admired figures.

Identification with caretakers is an automatic, unconscious mental process whereby an individual seeks to become like another person in one or several aspects. It naturally accompanies maturation and mental development and aids in the acquisition of values and ideals. Identifying with loved or admired figures is a way of securing the relationship, of bringing that person permanently close to oneself. Sociologically, such loved or admired figures are role models, but the ego ideal is an image inside the person. Ideals develop through identification with role models. As a guide to behavior, the superego helps bring about stability and consistency of performance. With its capacity to induce guilt and inspire behavior, the superego defines acceptable ways in which we may express ourselves and serves as a positively motivating force. When we live up to the demands of our superegos, we are rewarded by feelings of self-acceptance and self-worth. When we fall short of them, our self-esteem diminishes.

In addition to internal forces, every person must deal with the external environment. The environment can be a source of support and security. It is also a source of threat and frustration. Survival requires that we adapt to the environment. For example, we obey traffic signs, make a living, and pay taxes. External demands impinge on the self. We learn from or internalize these demands. This process of internalization was how Freud originally theorized superego formation. The conflict between "what I want to do" and "what I should do" is now inside the self. For example, most of us have sexual needs. These are internal needs. Society usually says a married person should not commit adultery. Conforming to that expectation is an external demand. The person may meet the social norm. But if the spouse cannot meet the person's sexual needs, the person now has an internal conflict.

The *ego* is another part of self, the part that keeps the superego, the id, and the environment in balance so that a person can function effectively. The ego regulates the drives, controls their expression in keeping with the superego, and directs the person to act upon the environment. The ego maintains self-control and tests reality. It includes functions such as memory, perception, judgment, attention, and abstract thinking. Like the superego, it normally develops as the child matures biologically and socially.

The ego acts on the basis of the reality principle: "What are the long-term consequences of this behavior?" When an impulse arises, a well-functioning ego will contain the impulse until, in effect, it has checked with the superego and memory to determine the consequences of enacting the impulse. The ego must contain, refine, or redirect the impulses so that the integrity of the personality is preserved. The ego is always mediating between the id and the superego—and also between these parts of the self and the environment. The term active coping" refers to *how* the ego mediates among these forces. An individual's coping style can be active or passive.

History of the Theory of Active Coping

The theory of active coping (see also the previous section) was first developed by Joel Shanan and derives from the ideas of David Rapaport,[3] and Carl Rogers,[4] and other "ego" and "self" psychologists. As noted in appendix A, Rappaport viewed the ego as a part of the personality, a part that began—and had the potential to remain—conflict free. This view deviated from Freud's more pessimistic view, which held that the individual's inherent needs, particularly sexuality and aggression, inevitably conflicted with socialization into civilization. In contrast to Freud's focus on biological (sex, eating, self-preservation) needs, Rogers focused on a wider array of growth-oriented needs and desires, emphasizing the importance of a child's caretakers in providing unconditional acceptance and encouraging the child's exploration and self-development.

Shanan, a survivor of the Holocaust, immigrated after World War II to Israel from Austria. In the 1950s, he studied at the University of Chicago on the Committee on Human Development with other psychologists interested in understanding adult development and creativity. Shanan eventually integrated the ideas of ego psychology and the self-developmental perspective of Rogers—the essential role of the caretaker in giving an individual a sense of self and identity—to formulate the theory of active coping. As a professor at Hebrew University, he taught my mentor, Jordan Jacobowitz.

Jacobowitz, doing his graduate studies in psychology abroad in Israel, initially worked for Shanan as an assistant in selecting candidates for enrollment in the medical school at the Hebrew University Hadassah Hospital. While using various psychological tests to evaluate the coping styles of candidates, he noted that different tests occasionally yielded conflicting measurements of these coping tendencies as well as other personality characteristics. He noted that these variations in scores between different tests fell into certain identifiable patterns, which he considered to be representative of different personality "types."

Notes

Introduction

1. The two studies are hereafter referred to the "Booth Studies." The articles reporting some of the findings include Leslie Pratch and Jordan Jacobowitz, "Gender, Motivation, and Coping in the Evaluation of Leadership Effectiveness," *Consulting Psychology Journal: Practice and Research* 48, no. 4 (1996): 203–220; and Leslie Pratch and Jordan Jacobowitz, "Integrative Capacity in the Evaluation of Leadership," *Journal of Applied Behavioral Research* (Summer 1998).

2. Formal studies and routine follow-ups with my clients reveal that indicators from the assessments exceed 98 percent accuracy in predicting an executive's performance if the candidate is hired. I have not followed up on the performance of executives I have assessed who were not hired.

1. The Power of Active Coping

1. See Leslie Pratch and Jordan Jacobowitz, "The Psychology of Leadership in Rapidly Changing Conditions," *Genetic, Social, and General Psychology Monographs* (Summer 1997), for the original article delineating the theory and methodology associated with a structural psychological assessment. The article provides the definition of the term "active coping" as used

by Joel Shanan in the 1950s and 1960s in research he and his colleagues conducted in Israel. His definition differs from mine. I have developed my own construct, presented in this book based on his and others' thinking.

2. I use the term "executive" to refer to the status of any person occupying an executive office in a managerial hierarchy. I also use the term "leader" to refer to individuals who occupy leadership roles, whether or not they are executives.

3. See Pratch and Jacobowitz, "The Psychology of Leadership," 169–196.

4. There are other elements that are important in some cases but not as important in other, for example, self-esteem. Self-esteem is a reflection of self-confidence, self-respect, and self-worth.

5. See Leslie Pratch, "Integrity in Business Executives," *Journal of Private Equity* (December 2009): 1–14.

6. See Leslie Pratch and Jordan Jacobowitz, "Optimal Psychological Autonomy and Its Implications for Selecting Portfolio CEOs," *Journal of Private Equity* (December 2007): 53–70.

7. See Pratch and Jacobowitz, "Integrative Capacity."

8. For examples, see Robert J. Ellis, "Self-Monitoring and Leadership Emergence in Groups," *Personality and Social Psychology Bulletin* 14 (1988): 681–693; Lori Katz and Seymour Epstein, "Constructive Thinking and Coping with Laboratory-Induced Stress," *Journal of Personality and Social Psychology* 61, no. 5 (1991): 789–800; David A. Kenny and Stephen J. Zaccaro, "An Estimate of Variance Due to Traits in Leadership," *Journal of Applied Psychology* 68 (1993); Robert G. Lord, C. L. DeVader, and G. M. Alliger, "A Meta-Analysis of the Relation Between Personality Traits and Leadership Perceptions: An Application of Validity Generalization Procedures," *Journal of Applied Psychology* 61 (1986): 402–410.

9. For instance, see George. O. Klemp and David C. McClelland, "What Characterizes Intelligent Functioning Among Senior Managers?" in *Practical Intelligence: Nature and Origin of Competence in the Everyday World*, ed. Robert J. Sternberg and Richard. K. Wagner (Cambridge: Cambridge University Press, 1986), 31–50; Gary Yukl, *Leadership in Organizations* (Englewood Cliffs, N.J.: Prentice-Hall, 1994).

10. The five-factor model of John M. Digman, "Personality Structure: Emergence of the Five-Factor Model," *Annual Review of Psychology* 4 (1990): 417–440, for instance, is a model of personality traits. It relates to the structure of trait words. At most, it tells us something about human social perception and information processing.

11. Numerous studies have revealed correlations between active coping and adaptation in a wide range of settings, such as medical school, adjustment to a new culture, and maintaining mental health under taxing

conditions (reviewed in Joel Shanan, "Coping Styles and Coping Strategies in Later Life," in *Clinical and Scientific Psychogeriatrics*, vol. 1: *The Holistic Approaches*, ed. Manfred Berenger and Sanfred Finkle [New York: Springer, 1990], 76–111).

12. Positive correlations between power and achievement motivations and successful organizational leadership have been reported for many years in a wide variety of settings. See, for example, David C. McClelland, "The Achievement Motive," in *Motivation and Personality: Handbook of Thematic Content Analysis*, ed. Charles P. Smith (Cambridge: Cambridge University Press, 1992), 393–400; and David G. Winter, "Leader Appeal, Leader Performance, and the Motive Profiles of Leaders and Followers," *Journal of Personality and Social Psychology* 52 (1987): 196–202.

2. Predicting Performance

1. For references, see J. P. Campbell, "The Definition and Measurement of Performance in the New Age," in *The Changing Nature of Performance*, ed. Daniel R. Ilgen and Elaine D. Pulakos (San Francisco: Jossey-Bass, 1999), 399–401; and F. L. Schmidt and J. E. Hunter, "The Utility and Validity of Personnel Selection in Psychology: Practical Implications of Eighty-Five Years of Research Findings," *Psychological Bulletin* 124 (1988): 262–274.

2. In statistics, a correlation coefficient of .5 means that one-quarter of the variability is explained by the data. In other words, past performance explains at most about one-quarter of future performance; 75 percent of the variance remains unexplained. This statistic might mean that if you rely only on past performance for hiring executives in the top 10 percent of the business hierarchy, you would be not be picking absolutely the best executive approximately three times out of four. Of course, you do not always need the best executive. The second and third best might still do the job. But for some situations, only the best will work.

Nevertheless, as I have mentioned before, those who weigh in on hiring decisions tend to focus on experience, credentials, and other factors from the past, all of which hopeful job candidates may "spin" or even distort. Interviews and reference checks examine candidates' past achievements and may miss qualities that would be valuable under new circumstances. Moreover, executives likely merely to be considered by investors or board members have well-documented records of excellence. Those with evident weaknesses in their job histories have long since been weeded out. The winnowing that first brings executives to the attention of individuals charged with hiring or investment decisions (e.g., executive recruiters and industry contacts) means that superficially, at least, all surviving candidates will *appear* good on paper.

3. Some of the classical or earlier literature on this topic includes the work of Jack Block. Jack Block studied children in a very long longitudinal study. The children grew up in California. The original book was *Lives Through Time* (Berkeley, Calif.: Bancroft, 1971). That same population was studied further when they reached middle age (Block had studied them through their twenties). That book was *Present and Past in Middle Life* by Dorothy H. Eichorn and colleagues (Hillsdale, N.J.: Academic Press, 1981). Jack Block also looked at that population in old age as well as summarizing the major findings.

Another source is the work of George E. Vaillant, both in his book *Adaptation to Life* (Cambridge, Mass.: Harvard University Press, 1977) and *The Wisdom of the Ego* (Cambridge, Mass.: Harvard University Press, 1993). Those books focus on "coping" via "defense mechanisms" and include a number of developmental studies that followed people either retrospectively or prospectively from childhood to middle or late adulthood. Vaillant's *Triumphs of Experience: The Men of the Harvard Grant Study* (Cambridge, Mass.: Harvard University Press, 2013) is his latest, and, I assume, last book following up the Harvard college students (all men), who were now in their nineties. This book also contains the latest findings from two other very long longitudinal studies from childhood and/or adolescence onwards: The Glueck Study of lower- to middle-class men and the Terman study of gifted (high-IQ) women. Although findings were very complex, Vaillant argued that having "warm families" as children was one of the key predictors of success and happiness throughout life. As he put it: the "most important influence by far on a flourishing life is love." (To define a "flourishing life" he used the summation of ten variables, among them: "being listed in Who's Who in America," "earning income in the study's top quartile," and "having a good marriage.") (One caveat was that men who became alcoholics, independent of their childhood experiences, had poor life outcomes. These men, however, according to Vaillant had a family history of alcoholism.)

There is a long-term longitudinal study on fifty-four children in Topeka, beginning in infancy and moving through adulthood. A series of books have been written about them, including Sibylle K. Escalona and Grace M. Heider's *Prediction and Outcome: A Study in Child Development* (New York: Basic Books, 1960), Riley W. Gardner and Alice E. Moriarty's *Personality Development at Preadolescence* (Seattle: University of Washington Press, 1968), and Lois Murphy's *Widening World of Childhood* (New York: Basic Books, 1962).

In clinical populations, David Gutmann made connections between child-hood and adulthood (and even later adulthood) in, for example, in *Reclaimed Powers* (Evanston, Ill.: Northwestern University Press, 1994). Also, Jordan Jacobowitz and Nancy Newton recorded connections in "Time, Context, and Character: A Life-span View of Psychopathology During the Second Half of Life," in *New Dimensions in Adult Development*, ed. Robert A. Nemiroff and Calvin A. Colarusso (New York: Basic Books, 1990), 306–332.

Popular documentaries include *Boyhood* and the *7 Up* series, for example, *35 Up*.

4. A note about evaluating the accuracy of probabilistic predictions: It is rarely possible to compare one method to other methods in controlled stud-ies. The best one can do is conduct longitudinal field studies, as I continue to do in my research, to determine whether predictions bear out over time, and when they do not, to investigate why and make appropriate modifications to improve future predictions. That is the essence of an empirically oriented clinical approach.

5. Managerial studies suggest that effective executive leadership depends on the ability to respond in an adaptive manner to emergent, dynamic, and complex situations. For other examples, see S. Carroll and D. J. Gillen, "Are the Classical Management Functions Useful in Describing Managerial Work?" *Academy of Management Review* 12 (1987): 38–51; J. P. Kotter, "What Leaders Really Do," *Harvard Business Review* (May/June 1990): 103–111; W. Skinner and W. E. Sasser, "Managers with Impact: Versa-tile and Inconsistent," *Harvard Business Review* 55, no. 6 (November/December 1977): 140–148; H. A. Simon, "Making Management Decisions: The Role of Intuition and Emotion," *Academy of Management Executive* (February 1987): 57–63; and R. Whitley, "On the Nature of Managerial Tasks and Skills: Their Distinguishing Characteristics and Organization," *Journal of Management Studies* 26, no. 3 (1989): 209–224.

3. Coping Styles and Coping Holes

1. See David Gutmann, "Psychological Development and Pathology in Later Adulthood," in *New Dimensions in Adult Development*, ed. Robert A. Nemiroff and Calvin A. Colarusso (New York: Basic Books, 1990), 170–185; and Michael Reynolds, *The Young Hemingway* (New York: Norton, 1986).

2. See, for example, the biographies of Hemingway by Michael Reynolds, particularly *Hemingway: The Final Years* (New York: Norton, 1999).

3. See Gutmann, "Psychological Development and Pathology in Later Adulthood," for an interesting account of Hemingway's adult onset of psychopathology.

4. If I had assessed him before the venture firm hired him, I might have anticipated the potential to lie. His lying, by the way, was yet another reason I began to focus on integrity as the first element of a coping style.

5. See John Colville, "The Personality of Sir Winston Churchill," in *Winston Churchill: Resolution, Defiance, Magnanimity, Good Will*, ed. R. Crosby Kemper II (Columbia: University of Missouri Press, 1995), 108–125, who describes Churchill's episodes of depression.

4. What Lies Beneath?

1. The projective techniques I use are not the only ones in use. There are others, the most famous probably being the Rorschach. To discuss the advantages of one against the other would go beyond the scope of this book, but see, for example, D. Rapaport, M. Gill, and R. Schafer, *Psychological Diagnostic Testing* (Madison, Conn.: International Universities Press, 1968).

2. L. Pratch and J. Jacobowitz, "Successful CEOs of Private-Equity Funded Ventures," *Journal of Private Equity* (Summer 2004): 8–31.

3. Although the character in Sandy's last story succeeds, it also suggests insecurity about that success. His insecurity suggests that perhaps even his success did not fully satisfy him.

4. The image of Rosa Parks fits our description of LHH. I am not saying that this was the real Rosa Parks but rather the image the country got of her.

5. Integrity

1. Erikson's idea of "identity" was another way of looking at integrity. In that regard integrity was seen as the meaning persons gave to their lives and selves as related to society and history. The integrative/synthesizing "self" or ego in active coping theory is an area for future thought.

2. The lack of integrity shown by some leading executives of financial institutions had a very bad effect on their companies and may have contributed to the bubble that led to the financial crisis of 2008 and the larger recession that followed.

3. The following description, from William Makepeace Thackeray's novel *Vanity Fair* (1848), is a good example of self-esteem without integrity: "Which of us is there can tell how much vanity lurks in our warmest regard for others, and how selfish our love is? Old Osborne did not speculate much on the mingled nature of his feelings, and how his instinct and selfishness were combating together. He firmly believed that everything he did was right, and that he ought on all occasions to have his own way—and like the sting of a wasp or serpent his hatred rushed out armed and poisonous against anything like opposition. He was proud of his hatred as of everything else. Always to be right, always to trample forward, and never to doubt, are not these the great qualities with which dulness takes a lead in the world?"

4. By agency costs, I mean both the cost if executives use organizational resources for their own benefit and the cost of techniques used to prevent that from happening.

5. We all recognize that some values are superior to others (e.g., not committing murder is superior to not stealing).

6. Iris Murdoch, "The Sublime and the Good," in *Existentialists and Mystics: Writings on Philosophy and Literature*, comp. Peter Conradi (New York: Allen Lane/Penguin, 1998), 215.

7. This does not mean that executives who have had such attachments always grow up with integrity, only that they are more likely to do so. We have no meaningful statistical data to state how much more likely.

8. When the parent's behavior is inconsistent or the child's temperament and inner resources are limited, the active coping style may not develop evenly across its four dimensions. A person's overt behavior may indicate an active orientation and conventional values, but the person's inner thoughts and feelings may be passively inclined. Such a person is a pseudocoper who has learned to present a façade of active behavior and rectitude while harboring buried resentments, hostilities, self-centered fantasies, or passive-dependent yearnings. Over time, the observed activity and good behaviors fade, and the latent passive, angry, rebellious, self-centered, or antisocial tendencies emerge. These are especially likely to appear in response to emotionally charged stressors or disappointments. Under such circumstances, pseudocopers may engage in low-integrity behavior, as when executives feel entitled to embezzle whatever they perceive to be rightfully theirs.

9. This selection is not a scientific one; I had not kept all of the test records of the executives I had assessed because I did not know I later would want to do any research with this material. I only began keeping my records around 2002. I only began keeping records systematically in conjunction with a spreadsheet that enabled me to enter scores and comments when I began the research for my article "Successful CEOs of Private Equity Funded

Ventures," *Journal of Private Equity* (Summer 2004): 8–31, and therefore my systematic records go back to 2004.

10. John Raven et al., *Manual for Raven's Progressive Matrices and Vocabulary Scales: Section 4* (London: Oxford Psychologists Press, 1988).

11. The standard deviation on the APM in a population of high-achieving executives is 4. High-integrity executives scored 1.5 standard deviations higher than the low integrity executives.

12. This is consistent with Lawrence Kohlberg's stage model view of the development of moral reasoning. See his "The Development of Children's Orientation Towards a Moral Order: I. Sequence in the Development of Moral Thought," *Vita Humana* 6 (1963): 11–33. Kohlberg proposed a model of moral development that consisted of three phases emerging at predictable points in a child's maturation. Kohlberg called the first phase "preconventional morality." This phase characterizes early to middle childhood. Children behave well either to avoid punishment or be rewarded. Moral reasoning in this phase follows the reality principle, minimizing pain and maximizing pleasure in the context of social and physical reality.

Kohlberg called the second phase "conventional morality." This phase typically begins in middle childhood and extends to early adolescence. At this level, one behaves well to maintain proper relationships with others or to follow the accepted rules and regulations of one's society.

Kohlberg's called the third phase, occurring in adulthood, "post-conventional morality." During this phase, the individual is freed of rigid authority and learns to fashion a personal code of ethics using abstract reasoning rather than automatically capitulating to convention. The individual can justify moral decisions in terms of prevailing social ideals, such as specific individual rights, or universal concepts, such as justice. The person who attains this level of moral reasoning can determine what is right in any particular set of unique circumstances. He can choose to defy prevailing rules when those norms conflict with his own ethical sense.

13. I did not separate organizational factors and the active coping tendencies of the low-integrity executives. But this is beside the point. Lower-integrity executives were put into the low-integrity group for their individual behaviors, for failing the tests of transparency and commitment. Their personality tendencies, then, not the characteristics of the organizations they joined, become the key explanatory variable in explaining their low integrity.

14. This test was standardized with an American adult male population. It consists of twenty motivational scales and two validity scales. Each motivational scale represents a defined psychological need such as the need to achieve, to socialize, to direct others, or to have fun. The validity scales

assess tendencies to respond in a haphazard fashion and to represent the self in either an extremely negative or positive fashion.

6. Psychological Autonomy: Lemmings Need Not Apply

1. I. L. Janis, *Victims of Groupthink* (Boston: Houghton Mifflin, 1972).

2. See E. P. Hollander, "Conformity, Status, and Idiosyncrasy Credit," *Psychological Review* 65 (1958): 117–127.

3. See J. A. Conger and R. N. Kanungo, *Charismatic Leadership* (San Francisco: Jossey-Bass, 1988).

4. See C. J. Cox et al., "Toward a Behavioral Theory of Charismatic Leadership in Organizational Settings," *Academy of Management* 12, no. 4 (1987): 637–647; E. Hunter and A. M. Jordan, "An Analysis of Qualities Associated with Leadership Among College Students," *Journal of Educational Psychology* 30 (1939): 497–509.; H. M. Richardson and N. G. Hanawalt, "Leadership as Related to the Bernreuter Personality Measures: III. Leadership Among Men in Vocational and Social Activities," *Journal of Social Psychology* 36 (1952): 141–153. For reviews, see B. M. Bass, "From Transactional to Transformational Leadership: Learning to Share the Vision," *Organizational Dynamics* 18, no. 3 (1990): 19–31; and Gary Yukl, *Leadership in Organizations*, 5th ed. (Englewood Cliffs, N.J.: Prentice-Hall, 2001).

5. A. Zaleznik, "Managers and Leaders: Are They Different?" *Harvard Business Review* (May–June 1977).

6. A. Zaleznik, "The Leadership Gap," *Journal of the Academy of Management* 4, no. 1 (1990): 11.

7. According to the ego psychology school of psychoanalytic theory, healthy adaptation and growth depend on the availability of free energy for use by the ego for well-adapted inner- and outer-directed action for active, autonomous coping. Excessive restraint of the drives through defensive mechanisms depletes the energy available to the ego and makes it reliant on external factors to direct it. A relative lack of successful restraint of the drives, however, leads to dependency on the drives and usually excessive independence from the environment. In either case, the person passively yields to external or internal demands. By contrast, the active coper is able to maintain control of inner drives without excessive expenditure of energy available to the ego and can thereby interact with the environment in an involved, realistic, and self-directed manner.

7. Integrative Capacity:
Seeing Reality with Both Eyes Open

1. See J. K. Hemphill and A. E. Coons, "Development of the Leader Behavior Description Questionnaire," in *Leader Behavior: Its Description and Measurement*, ed. Ralph M. Stogdill and A. E. Coons (Columbus: Bureau of Business Research, Ohio State University, 1957).

2. See D. A. Kenny and S. J. Zaccaro, "An Estimate of Variance Due to Traits in Leadership," *Journal of Applied Psychology* 68 (1993).

3. From a letter to Albert G. Hodges, April 4, 1864.

4. The Emancipation Proclamation only freed slaves in the rebel states.

5. The fact that his father had painted over the window did not mean he did not see reality with both eyes open. I know nothing about his father other than that he built a successful company that needed Mike's help.

8. Catalytic Coping

1. Kranz was first made a flight director during the Gemini program and first performed the so-called operations shift (the active duty role of flight director) during Gemini 4. He served as flight director on odd-numbered Apollo missions through the final mission, Apollo 17. Apollo 1 was originally named AS-204, one of a series of AS (Apollo Saturn) flights and was later renamed Apollo 1 to honor the astronauts who died in the fire. There are no missions called Apollo 2 and Apollo 3. Apollo missions 5, 7, 9, and 11 were successful, with Apollo 11 being the first moon landing. Apollo 13 turned critical failure into life-saving success. Apollo 15 and 17 were successful missions to the moon.

2. S. W. Sears, *To The Gates of Richmond: The Peninsula Campaign* (New York: Houghton-Mifflin, 2001).

3. J. E. Smith, *Grant* (New York: Simon & Schuster, 2001), 201.

4. Both B. D. Simpson, *Ulysses S. Grant: Triumph Over Adversity* (Houghton Mifflin Harcourt, 2000), 61; and Smith, *Grant*, agree, as do all Grant biographers with whom I'm familiar, that Grant had a drinking problem when he resigned from the army in California in 1854, compounded by loneliness, boredom, and ill health.

Neither Simpson nor Smith finds any situation in which Grant's military performance was hampered by alcohol. Both authors say that Grant was watched like a hawk by his adjutant, Col. John Rawlins, a vehement teetotaler.

Simpson says, in reference to a report of Grant's drinking early in the war: "And so Ulysses S. Grant realized he would never fully leave his past behind him. Any time he offended someone, that someone was sure to whisper that the general was a drunkard. In fact, although Grant occasionally consumed alcoholic beverages, there was no cause for alarm. At best his spells of sickness (and the treatments prescribed for them) lent some credence to those tales. Rawlins, whose fierce commitment to abstinence was already becoming legendary, expressed no objection to the medicinal use of alcohol. However, he concluded that henceforth he must protect Grant from the temptations of alcohol, because even a drink or two would tend to substantiate rumors of a bender—and Lincoln and other top administration officials would keep an ear open to such reports" (108).

Smith, in his biography, finds some truth in rumors of Grant's wartime drinking. But, maintaining that Rawlins ensured that Grant never drank during important movements or operations, he concludes: "As a journalist who covered Grant's campaigns wrote: 'It can be safely asserted that no officer or civilian ever saw any open drinking at General Grant's headquarters from Cairo to Appomattox. This was wholly and solely the result of Rawlins' uncompromising attitude, and Grant's acquiescence in what he knew to be for his own good'" (232).

The phrase "Cairo to Appomattox" comprises Grant's entire Civil War military career.

5. The first chapter of Horace Porter's memoir *Campaigning with Grant* gives the most personal and revealing account of Grant in action: Facing a nearly impossible situation, assuming command of a starving army surrounded and besieged in Chattanooga, he arrives on the scene and in a few hours assesses the situation and issues a few terse orders that set in motion events that led to one of the Union's most crushing and unlikely victories, Shiloh.

6. See J. M. McPherson, *This Mighty Scourge: Perspectives on the Civil War* (New York: Oxford University Press, 2007), esp. 110–115, which gives a pretty good sense of Grant's salient characteristics as a general: his calmness under pressure; his ability to size up a situation quickly; and his decisiveness, clarity of expression, physical and moral courage, and "sense of self."

7. Michael Korda, *IKE: An American Hero* (New York: HarperCollins, 2009), 368.

8. See James R. Arnold, *Grant Wins the War: Decision at Vicksburg* (Hoboken, N.J.: John Wiley & Sons, 1997), 201.

9. Smith, *Grant*, 116.

10. Ibid.

11. McPherson, *This Mighty Scourge*, 111.

12. That point is made in S. W. Sears, *Landscape Turned Red* (New York: Houghton-Mifflin, 1983), the authoritative study of the Antietam campaign.

9. Implications for Female Leaders

1. Claire Cain Miller, "For Incoming IBM Chief, Self-Confidence Is Rewarded," *New York Times* (October 27, 2011).

2. For readers interested in further information, see the complete article reporting the study: L. Pratch and J. Jacobowitz, "Gender, Motivation, and Coping in the Evaluation of Leadership Effectiveness," *Consulting Psychology Journal: Practice and Research* 48, no. 4 (1996): 203–220.

3. Bakan, a social scientist, identified the communal and agentic styles. D. Bakan, *The Duality of Human Existence* (Chicago: Rand McNally, 1966).

4. See, for example, J. K. Hemphill and A. E. Coons, "Development of the Leader Behavior Description Questionnaire," in *Leader Behavior: Its Description and Measurement*, ed. R. M. Stogdill and A. E. Coons (Columbus: Bureau of Business Research, Ohio State University, 1957); and R. M. Stogdill and C. L. Shartle, *Methods in the Study of Administrative Leadership* (Columbus: Ohio State University, Bureau of Business Research, 1956).

10. Past Is Not Necessarily Prologue: Improving Your Active Coping

1. This attitude is more common in old family businesses than it is in publicly traded corporations.

2. K. Blanchard and S. Johnson, *The One-Minute Manager* (New York: William Morrow & Company, 1982).

12. Developing Active Coping: A Success Story

1. His point of view is consistent with that put forth in chapter 1, describing the differences between current state and developmental models of personality.

Appendix A: Technical Companion to Chapter 3

1. See H. English and A. English, *A Comprehensive Dictionary of Psychological and Psychoanalytic Terms* (New York: Longmans, Green, 1958).

2. Valence, as used in psychology, means the intrinsic attractiveness (positive valence) or aversiveness (negative valence) of an event, object, or situation.

3. In 1958, Marie Jahoda published an important article on the theory of "Ideal Mental Health." M. Jahoda, "Current Concepts of Positive Mental Health," in *Encyclopedia of Sociology*, ed. Edgar F. Borgatta (1958; repr. New York: Macmillan Library Reference, 2000).

4. S. Freud, Sigmund. "An Outline of Psychoanalysis." In *The Standard Edition of the Complete Psychological Works of Sigmund Freud*, vol. 23, ed. James Strachey. London: Hogarth, 1940), 15; this page can be read in the original German in Freud's *Gesammelte Werke* 17:67.

5. H. Hartmann, *Ego Psychology and the Problem of Adaptation*, trans. David Rappaport (New York: International Universities Press, 1958).

6. E. Erikson, *Identity, Youth, and Crisis*, Austen Riggs Monograph 7 (New York: Norton, 1968).

7. D. Rapaport, "The Theory of Ego Autonomy: A Generalization," in *The Collected Papers of David Rapaport*, ed. Merton Gill (New York: Basic Books, 1957), 541.

8. These authors included T. C. Kroeber, "The Coping Functions of the Ego Mechanisms," in *The Study of Lives*, ed. R. W. White (New York: Atherton, 1963); N. Haan, *Coping and Defending: Processes of Self-Environment Organization* (New York: Academic Press, 1977); and G. Vaillant, *Adaptation to Life* (Cambridge, Mass.: Harvard University Press, 1977).

9. D. Gutmann, *Reclaimed Powers* (Evanston, Ill.: Northwestern University Press, 1994).

10. R. Lazarus and S. Folkman, *Stress, Appraisal, and Coping* (New York: Springer, 1984).

11. J. Shanan, *Personality Types and Culture in Later Adulthood* (Basel: Karger, 1985), 121–232.

Appendix B: Technical Companion to Chapter 4

1. They are also easier for candidates who are already in contention for senior leadership roles to project the image that he or she thinks the society and a board of directors want to see.

2. For example, see J. Jacobowitz, "The Prediction of Performance in Medical School," Unpublished master's thesis (Hebrew University of Jerusalem, 1976).

3. D. Rapaport, "The Autonomy of the Ego," "Some Metapsychological Considerations Concerning Activity and Passivity," and "The Theory of Ego Autonomy: A Generalization," all in *The Collected Papers of David Rapaport*, ed. Merton Gill (New York: Basic Books, 1957).

4. C. Rogers, *On Becoming a Person: A Therapist's View of Psychotherapy* (Boston: Houghton Mifflin, 1961).

Bibliography

Apted, Michael. *35 Up.* 1991. http://www.imdb.com/title/tto101254/?ref
_=fn_al_tt_1.

Arnold, James R. *Grant Wins the War: Decision at Vicksburg.* Hoboken,
N.J.: John Wiley & Sons, 1997.

Bakan, D. *The Duality of Human Existence.* Chicago: Rand McNally, 1966.

Bass, Bernard M. *Bass and Stogdill's Handbook of Leadership: A Survey of
Theory and Research.* New York: Free Press, 1990.

——. "From Transactional to Transformational Leadership: Learning to
Share the Vision." *Organizational Dynamics* 18, no. 3 (1990): 19–31.

Blanchard, Kenneth, and Spencer Johnson. *The One-Minute Manager.* New
York: William Morrow & Company, 1982.

Block, Jack. *Lives Through Time.* Berkeley, Calif.: Bancroft, 1971.

Campbell, John P. "The Definition and Measurement of Performance in the
New Age." In *The Changing Nature of Performance,* ed. Daniel R. Ilgen
and Elaine D. Pulakos, 399–401. San Francisco: Jossey-Bass, 1999.

Carroll, Stephen, and Dennis J. Gillen. "Are the Classical Management
Functions Useful in Describing Managerial Work?" *Academy of Management Review* 12 (1987): 38–51.

Chhokar, Jagdeep S., Felix Brodbeck, and Robert J. House, eds. *Culture and
Leadership Across the World: The GLOBE Book of In-Depth Studies of
Twenty-Five Societies.* New York: Taylor & Francis, 2007.

Colville, John. "The Personality of Sir Winston Churchill." In *Winston Churchill: Resolution, Defiance, Magnanimity, Good Will*, ed. R. Crosby Kemper II, 108–125. Columbia: University of Missouri Press, 1995.

Conger, Jay A., and Rabindra N. Kanungo. *Charismatic Leadership*. San Francisco: Jossey-Bass, 1988.

Cox, Charles J., Jay A. Conger, and Rabindra N. Kanungo. "Toward a Behavioral Theory of Charismatic Leadership in Organizational Settings." *Academy of Management* 12, no. 4 (1987): 637–647.

Digman, John M. "Personality Structure: Emergence of the Five-Factor Model." *Annual Review of Psychology* 4 (1990): 417–440.

Eichorn, Dorothy H., Paul H. Mussen, John A. Clausen, Norma Haan, and Marjorie P. Honzik. *Present and Past in Middle Life*. Hillsdale, N.J.: Academic Press, 1981.

Ellis, Robert J. "Self-Monitoring and Leadership Emergence in Groups." *Personality and Social Psychology Bulletin* 14 (1988): 681–693.

English, Horace, and Ava English. *A Comprehensive Dictionary of Psychological and Psychoanalytic Terms*. New York: Longmans, Green, 1958.

Erikson, Erik H. *Childhood and Society*. New York: Norton, 1963.

——. *Identity: Youth and Crisis*. Austen Riggs Monograph 7. New York: Norton, 1968.

Escalona, Sibylle K., and Grace Moore Heider. *Prediction and Outcome: A Study in Child Development*. New York: Basic Books, 1960.

Freud, Sigmund. "An Outline of Psychoanalysis." In *The Standard Edition of the Complete Psychological Works of Sigmund Freud*, vol. 23, ed. James Strachey. London: Hogarth, 1940.

——. *The Ego and the Id*. 1923; repr. New York: Norton: New York, 1989.

Gardner, Riley W., and Alice E. Moriarty. *Personality Development at Preadolescence: Explorations of Structure Formation*. Seattle: University of Washington Press, 1968.

Gilbert, Martin. *Churchill: A Study in Greatness*. London: Pimlico, 2001.

Goodwin, Doris K. *Team of Rivals*. New York: Simon & Schuster, 2005.

Guelzo, Allen C. *Lincoln's Emancipation Proclamation: The End of Slavery in America*. New York: Simon & Schuster, 2004.

Gutmann, David. "Psychological Development and Pathology in Later Adulthood." In *New Dimensions in Adult Development*, ed. Robert A. Nemiroff and Calvin A. Colarusso, 170–185. New York: Basic Books, 1990.

——. *Reclaimed Powers*. Evanston, Ill.: Northwestern University Press, 1994.

Haan, Norma. *Coping and Defending: Processes of Self-Environment Organization*. New York: Academic Press, 1977.

Hartmann, Heinz. "The Development of the Ego Concept in Freud's Work." *International Journal of Psychoanalysis* 37 (1956): 425–438.

——. *Ego Psychology and the Problem of Adaptation.* Trans. David Rappaport. New York: International Universities Press, 1958.

Hemphill, John K., and A. E. Coons. "Development of the Leader Behavior Description Questionnaire." In *Leader Behavior: Its Description and Measurement,* ed. Ralph M. Stogdill and A. E. Coons. Columbus: Bureau of Business Research, Ohio State University, 1957.

Hofstede, Geert, Gert Jan Hofstede, and Michael Minkov. *Cultures and Organizations: Software of the Mind.* New York: McGraw Hill, 2010.

Hollander, Edward P. "Conformity, Status, and Idiosyncrasy Credit." *Psychological Review* 65 (1958): 117–127.

Hunter, E. C., and A. M. Jordan. "An Analysis of Qualities Associated with Leadership Among College Students." *Journal of Educational Psychology* 30 (1939): 497–509.

Jacobowitz, Jordan. "The Prediction of Performance in Medical School." Unpublished master's thesis, Hebrew University of Jerusalem, Israel, 1976.

——. "Stability and Change of Coping Patterns During the Middle Years as a Function of Personality Type." Unpublished doctoral thesis, Hebrew University of Jerusalem, Israel, 1984.

Jacobowitz, Jordan, and Nancy Newton. "Time, Context, and Character: A Lifespan View of Psychopathology During the Second Half of Life." In *New Dimensions in Adult Development,* ed. Robert A. Nemiroff and Calvin A. Colarusso, 306–332. New York: Basic Books, 1990.

Jahoda, Marie. "Current Concepts of Positive Mental Health." In *Encyclopedia of Sociology,* ed. Edgar F. Borgatta. 1958; repr. New York: Macmillan Library Reference, 2000.

Janis, Irving L. *Crucial Decisions.* New York: Free Press, 1989.

——. "Groupthink." *Psychology Today* 5, no. 6 (November 1971).

——. *Victims of Groupthink.* Boston: Houghton Mifflin, 1972.

Katz, Lori, and Seymour Epstein. "Constructive Thinking and Coping with Laboratory-Induced Stress." *Journal of Personality and Social Psychology* 61, no. 5 (1991): 789–800.

Kenny, David A., and Stephen J. Zaccaro. "An Estimate of Variance Due to Traits in Leadership." *Journal of Applied Psychology* 68 (1993).

Klemp, George O., and David C. McClelland. "What Characterizes Intelligent Functioning Among Senior Managers?" In *Practical Intelligence: Nature and Origin of Competence in the Everyday World,* ed. Robert J. Sternberg and Richard. K. Wagner, 31–50. Cambridge: Cambridge University Press, 1986.

Kohlberg, Lawrence. "Continuities in Child and Adult Moral Development Revisited." In *Lifespan Developmental Psychology: Personality and Socialization*, ed. Paul Baltes and Klaus W. Schaie. New York: Academic Press, 1973.

——. "The Development of Children's Orientation Towards a Moral Order: I. Sequence in the Development of Moral Thought." *Vita Humana* 6 (1963): 11–33.

Kohut, Heinz. *The Analysis of the Self*. New York: International Universities Press, 1971.

——. *The Restoration of the Self*. New York: International Universities Press, 1977.

Korda, Michael. *IKE: An American Hero*. New York: HarperCollins, 2009.

Kotter, John P. "What Leaders Really Do." *Harvard Business Review* (May/June 1990): 103–111.

Kranz, Gene. *Failure Is Not an Option*. New York: Simon & Schuster, 2009.

Kroeber, T. C. "The Coping Functions of the Ego Mechanisms." In *The Study of Lives*, ed. Robert W. White. New York: Atherton, 1963.

Lazarus, Richard. S., and Susan Folkman. *Stress, Appraisal, and Coping*. New York: Springer, 1984.

Lord, Robert G., C. L. DeVader, and G. M. Alliger. "A Meta-Analysis of the Relation Between Personality Traits and Leadership Perceptions: An Application of Validity Generalization Procedures." *Journal of Applied Psychology* 61 (1986): 402–410.

McClelland, David C. "The Achievement Motive." In *Motivation and Personality: Handbook of Thematic Content Analysis*, ed. Charles P. Smith, 393–400. Cambridge: Cambridge University Press, 1992.

McPherson, James M. *This Mighty Scourge: Perspectives on the Civil War*. New York: Oxford University Press, Inc., 2007.

Miller, Claire Caine. "For Incoming IBM Chief, Self-Confidence is Rewarded." *New York Times* (October 27, 2011).

Murdoch, Iris. "The Sublime and the Good." In *Existentialists and Mystics: Writings on Philosophy and Literature*, comp. Peter Conradi, 205–220. New York: Allen Lane/Penguin, 1998.

Murphy, Lois B. *Widening World of Childhood: Paths Toward Mastery*. New York: Basic Books, 1962.

Murphy, Lois B., and Alice E. Moriarty. *Vulnerability, Coping, and Growth: From Infancy to Adolescence*. New Haven, Conn.: Yale University Press, 1976.

——. *Development, Vulnerability, and Resilience*. New Haven, Conn.: Yale University Press, 1976.

Porter, Horace. *Campaigning with Grant*. New York: The Century Co., 1897.

Pratch, Leslie. "Integrity in Business Executives." *Journal of Private Equity* (December 2009): 1–14.

——. "The Use of a Clinical Psychological Method to Predict Management Performance." *Journal of Private Equity* (December 2008): 1–25.

Pratch, Leslie, and Jordan Jacobowitz. "Gender, Motivation, and Coping in the Evaluation of Leadership Effectiveness." *Consulting Psychology Journal: Practice and Research* 48, no. 4 (1996): 203–220.

——. "Integrative Capacity in the Evaluation of Leadership." *Journal of Applied Behavioral Research* (Summer 1998).

——. "Optimal Psychological Autonomy and Its Implications for Selecting Portfolio CEOs." *Journal of Private Equity* (December 2007): 53–70.

——. "The Psychology of Leadership in Rapidly Changing Conditions: A Structural Psychological Approach." *Genetic, Social, and General Psychology Monographs* (Summer 1997).

——. "Successful CEOs of Private-Equity Funded Ventures." *Journal of Private Equity* (Summer 2004): 8–31.

Rapailli, Clotaire. *The Culture Code: An Ingenious Way People Around the World Live and Buy as They Do.* New York: Broadway, 2007.

Rapaport, David. "The Autonomy of the Ego." In *The Collected Papers of David Rapaport*, ed. Merton Gill, 357–367. New York: Basic Books, 1957.

——. "Some Metapsychological Considerations Concerning Activity and Passivity." In *The Collected Papers of David Rapaport*, ed. Merton Gill, 350–368. New York: Basic Books, 1957.

——. "The Theory of Ego Autonomy: A Generalization." In *The Collected Papers of David Rapaport*, ed. Merton Gill, 722–744. New York: Basic Books, 1957.

Rapaport, David, Merton Gill, and Roy Schafer. *Psychological Diagnostic Testing.* Madison, Conn.: International Universities Press, 1968.

Raven, John, et al. *Manual for Raven's Progressive Matrices and Vocabulary Scales: Section 4.* London: Oxford Psychologists Press, 1988.

Reynolds, Michael. "Ernest Hemingway, 1899–1961: A Brief Biography." In *A Historical Guide to Ernest Hemingway*, ed. Linda Wagner-Martin. New York: Oxford University Press, 2000.

——. *Hemingway: The Final Years.* New York: Norton, 1999.

——. *Hemingway: The Paris Years.* New York: Norton, 1989.

——. *The Young Hemingway.* New York: Norton, 1986.

Richardson, H. M., and N. G. Hanawalt. "Leadership as Related to the Bernreuter Personality Measures: III. Leadership Among Men in Vocational and Social Activities." *Journal of Social Psychology* 36 (1952): 141–153.

Rogers, Carl R. *On Becoming a Person: A Therapist's View of Psychotherapy.* Boston: Houghton Mifflin, 1961.

Schlesinger, Arthur M., Jr. *A Thousand Days.* Boston: Houghton-Mifflin, 1965.

Schmidt, F. L., and Hunter, J. E. "The Utility and Validity of Personnel Selection in Psychology: Practical Implications of Eighty-Five Years of Research Findings." *Psychological Bulletin* 124 (1988): 262–274.

Sears, Stephen W. *Landscape Turned Red.* New York: Houghton-Mifflin, 1983.

——. *To The Gates of Richmond: The Peninsula Campaign.* New York: Houghton-Mifflin, 2001.

Shanan, Joel. "Coping Behavior in Assessment of Complex Tasks." *Proceedings of the 17th International Congress of Applied Psychology*, vol. 1. Brussels: Editest, 1973.

——. "Coping Styles and Coping Strategies in Later Life." In *Clinical and Scientific Psychogeriatrics*, vol. 1, *The Holistic Approaches*, ed. Manfred Berenger and Sanfred Finkle, 76–111. New York: Springer, 1990.

——. *Personality Types and Culture in Later Adulthood.* Basel: Karger, 1985.

Simon, Herman A. "Making Management Decisions: The Role of Intuition and Emotion." *Academy of Management Executive* (February 1987): 57–63.

Simpson, Brooks D. *Ulysses S. Grant: Triumph Over Adversity.* Houghton Mifflin Harcourt, 2000.

Skinner, W., and W. E. Sasser. "Managers with Impact: Versatile and Inconsistent." *Harvard Business Review* 55, no. 6 (November/December 1977): 140–148.

Smith, Jean Edward. *Grant.* New York: Simon & Schuster, 2001.

Stogdill, Richard M., and A. E. Coons. "Editorial Comments." In *Leader Behavior: Its Description and Measurement*, ed. Richard M. Stogdill and A. E. Coons. Columbus: Ohio State University, Bureau of Business Research, 1957.

Stogdill, Richard M., and Carroll L. Shartle. *Methods in the Study of Administrative Leadership.* Columbus: Ohio State University, Bureau of Business Research, 1956.

Thackeray, William M. *Vanity Fair: A Novel Without a Hero.* London: Bradbury and Evans, 1848.

Tzu, Sun. *The Art of War.* New York: Delacorte, 1983.

Vaillant, George. *Adaption to Life.* Cambridge, Mass.: Harvard University Press, 1977.

——. "Theoretical Hierarchy of Adaptive Ego Mechanisms." *Archives of General Psychiatry* 24 (1971): 107–118.

——. *Triumphs of Experience: The Men of the Harvard Grant Study*. Cambridge, Mass.: Harvard University Press, 2013.

——. *The Wisdom of the Ego*. Cambridge, Mass.: Harvard University Press, 1993.

Whitley, R. "On the Nature of Managerial Tasks and Skills: Their Distinguishing Characteristics and Organization." *Journal of Management Studies* 26, no. 3 (1989): 209–224.

Willner, Ann R. *The Spellbinders: Charismatic Political Leadership*. New Haven, Conn.: Yale University Press, 1984.

Winston, Robert. *Childhood in Our Time*. 2000. http://www.imdb.com/title/tt0290348/plotsummary?ref_=tt_ov_pl.

Winter, David G. "Leader Appeal, Leader Performance, and the Motive Profiles of Leaders and Followers." *Journal of Personality and Social Psychology* 52 (1987): 196–202.

Yukl, Gary. *Leadership in Organizations*. 1st ed. Englewood Cliffs, N.J.: Prentice-Hall, 1994.

——. *Leadership in Organizations*. 5th ed. Englewood Cliffs, N.J.: Prentice-Hall, 2001.

Zaleznik, Abraham. "The Leadership Gap." *Journal of the Academy of Management* 4, no. 1 (1990): 9–15.

——. "Management of Disappointment." In *The Irrational Executive*, ed. Manfred Kets de Vries, 224–248. New York: International Universities Press, 1984.

——. "Managers and Leaders: Are They Different?" *Harvard Business Review* (May–June 1977).

Index

abrasive personality, 158

abstract reasoning, 95–96

active coping, 194, 207n1; adaptation and, 208n11; blind spot awareness through, 179; in business leaders, 18; circumstances causing weaknesses in, 78; constant state of readiness through, 19; defining, 16; developing qualities of, 161; dysfunctional loyalties and, 38; elements of, 9; in everyday life, 14–15; executives with personalities for, 9–10; flexibility of, 55, 57; four elements of, 19–24, 22; history of, 206; information integration in, 185–86; integrity with elements of, 81–82, 166; leadership influenced by, 30–31; leadership research in, 24; of low-integrity executives, 214n13; as ongoing process, 183; as passivity defense, 39–40; in personality, 166; problem response optimization in, 157; psychoanalytic insights and, 1; psychological ammunition from, 16–17; psychological qualities combined for, 156; self-assessment for developing, 155–57, 184–85; self-awareness in, 184; sentence completion test in, 200; skills and traits in, 24–26; of Steve and George, 72; successful resolution from, 16; teach and support others through, 17; Tim's change from passive to, 156–57; weaknesses managed in, 17, 56–57; as whole person characteristic, 25; women's higher, 148–49; workplace and life goals connected in, 172. *See also* catalytic coping; coping; passive coping

99–100; parental identification
lacking in, 102; self-interests
pursued by, 105
low integrity, 93–94

Mack (client), 48–50
male leaders, 149
management skills, 42–43
managerial reforms, 48–49
masculine image, 58–59
mastery: coping and, 195;
individuals learning, 15; sense
of, 15
McClellan, George B., 38, 124,
125; decisive action avoided
by, 139; enemy obsessions of,
142–43; hesitation to act under
pressure of, 33–34; open disdain
displayed by, 142; worst-case
scenario imagined by, 143
measurement process, 185
memories, 203
mental fortitude, 143–44
mental health, 63, 135
mentors, 175, 182–83, 188
Mike (client), 133–35
module 1 (aims and goals), 168;
ethical goals in, 170–71; goals
and potential threats linking in,
172–73, 177; personal and social
goals in, 170; professional goals
in, 169–70
module 2 (frustrations), 168–69;
goals and potential threats
linking in, 172–73, 177;
questions to ask in, 171–72
module 3 (catalytic coping), 169;
adaptive and flexible responses
in, 173–74; psychological
autonomy awareness gained
in, 174; social realm questions

in, 174; suboptimal decision
recognition in, 174–75
module 4 (self-esteem), 169, 176
modules, self-assessment,
168–69
momentum of warfare, 141–42
moral development, 214n12
moral quality, 80–81, 92–93
Moriarty, Alice E., 210n3
motivational orientation, 31
motivations, 2, 23; in coping style,
99; personal, 172–73; projective
techniques for coping and, 76;
psychological, 170; psychological
need and, 214n14
Motorola, 4, 5, 6
Murdoch, Iris, 86
Murphy, Lois, 194, 195
myths, 164

needs, of others, 98, 118
nonverbal communications, 140

objective assessment, 199–200
observable behavior, 76
obstacles, 141, 178
Ohio State studies, 147–48
operations shift, 216n1
outside pressures, 55
overt behavior, 195

paradigmatic themes, 67
parents: child's behavior influenced
by, 204, 213n8; George
internalizing aspects of, 118–19;
lower integrity executives
identification with, 102;
personality and relationship of,
64; strained relationship of, 55.
See also father
Parks, Rosa, 77, 212n4

Berkeley College